BEFORE YUU BUY THAT BUILDING

The Small Business Owner's Guide To Buying Commercial Real Estate

by

Raphael Enrique Collazo

BEFORE YOU BUY THAT BUILDING
The Small Business Owner's Guide to Buying Commercial Real Estate

Copyright © 2021 by Raphael Enrique Collazo

All rights reserved.
No part of this book may be reproduced or transmitted without written permission from the author.

ISBN 978-0-9993348-5-0

Printed in the USA by Amazon KDP

DOWNLOAD THE GUIDE TO FINDING THE BEST COMMERCIAL DEALS FOR FREE!!

READ THIS FIRST:

As a thank you for buying my book,
I'd like to give you the customized guide to finding the best commercial deals I created

100% FREE!

TO DOWNLOAD, GO TO:
https://bit.ly/2Q0y4MW

FOLLOW ME ON SOCIAL MEDIA!

YouTube: https://bit.ly/2ZtLV3j
Facebook: https://bit.ly/2Ya90rk
Instagram: @commercial_louisville

DEDICATION

There are so many people to thank for the completion of this book. The writing process is a team effort and without such a stellar one in my corner, I would have never reached the finish line.

First, I want to thank my family for constantly supporting me and my work. You have showed me what it means to live an honorable life and I'll be forever grateful to you.

Second, I'd like to thank my beautiful, smart, and confident fiancé Melanie. Since we met, you have been my biggest cheerleader. I love you with all my heart and I can't wait for what our future holds.

Finally, I'm proud to dedicate this book to the entrepreneurs who make our economy turn. Without your dedication, passion, and willingness to take risks, the *"American Dream"* as we know it would cease to exist.

All the best,

Raphael Collazo

TABLE OF CONTENTS

Dedication		5
Introduction		9
Chapter 1	Beginning Your Journey	13
Chapter 2	Setting Expectations	21
Chapter 3	Assembling Your Real Estate Advisory Team	27
Chapter 4	Identifying Commercial Lenders	41
Chapter 5	Determining Your Needs	51
Chapter 6	Finding Your New Property	59
Chapter 7	Drafting Your Purchase Agreement	65
Chapter 8	Negotiating The Purchase Contract	77
Chapter 9	Performing Due Diligence	83
Chapter 10	Working With Your Lender	101
Chapter 11	Addressing Pre-Closing Items	111
Chapter 12	Completing Your Build-Out	121
Chapter 13	Opening Your Doors!	125
Bio		131
Book Recommendations		133
Real Estate Terminology		137

INTRODUCTION

Welcome to the wonderful world of commercial real estate! It's an exciting industry and one that's an important part of the entrepreneurial journey. For many of you, this is not your first rodeo. You have likely been in business for some time, and you're now interested in acquiring a commercial property of your very own. Since becoming a commercial real estate agent in 2019, I've had the privilege of helping many entrepreneurs buy commercial real estate for their business use. As I worked with my clients, I realized just how little was known about the process. There are plenty of resources available for those interested in buying residential real estate. However, that's not the case for commercial real estate. In fact, many of the resources out there are intentionally vague and difficult to comprehend.

This is especially troubling because the process of identifying, assessing, and acquiring commercial real estate is complex. If navigated incorrectly, business owners stand to lose tens of thousands, if not hundreds of thousands of dollars in repairs, legal fees, time etc. My goal with this book is to significantly reduce the heartache and expense experienced by business owners who are interested in taking control of their own destiny. In this book, I have laid out a 13-step plan that will help you get from the starting gate to opening your doors as quickly and seamlessly as possible. The insights contained in this book include:

1) **Beginning Your Journey** – We will review the pros and cons of purchasing commercial property and determine if it's the right move for you and your business.

2) **Setting Expectations** – I will share insights on what to expect throughout the acquisition process and explain the items you should prepare prior to beginning your search.

3) **Assembling Your Real Estate Advisory Team** – We will learn how to recruit an all-star real estate team that will help you secure the best property for your business needs while protecting your best interests.

4) **Identifying Commercial Lenders** – We will highlight the strategies you can employ to identify several commercial lenders.

5) **Determining Your Needs** – We will get clear on your search criteria to ensure you're able to find a property that aligns with your business goals.

6) **Finding Your New Property** – We will highlight ways to identify and analyze potential opportunities so you can narrow your list and select your top choice.

7) **Drafting Your Purchase Agreement** – We will discuss various items to consider as you draft your purchase agreement.

8) **Negotiating the Purchase Contract** – We will provide strategies to negotiate the most favorable deal for your property acquisition.

9) **Performing Due Diligence** – We will provide a comprehensive overview of actions to take and questions to consider as you work through your due diligence process.

10) **Working With Your Lender** - We will highlight the commercial lending process and explain how to streamline the process of securing your commercial loan.

11) **Addressing Pre-Closing Items** – We will specify various items you need to address prior to closing on your new commercial property.

12) **Completing Your Build Out** – We will explain how to work with your commercial contractor to ensure your build-out is completed on time and on budget.

13) **Opening Your Doors** – You have finally made it to the finish line! In this section, we will explain how to create systems to ensure you meet your real estate obligations and set yourself up for future business success.

At the end of each chapter, I'll provide action items to follow that will help you move the ball down the field. Through taking decisive action, you will gain knowledge and develop the skills necessary to navigate the pitfalls inherent in the commercial real estate acquisition process. Are you ready to begin your journey of buying your new commercial property? If so, let's begin.

CHAPTER 1
BEGINNING YOUR JOURNEY

"You don't have to be great to start, but you have to start to be great." – **Zig Ziglar**

The purpose of this book is to provide you with a framework for purchasing commercial property with expedience and without heartache. However, before taking the plunge, it's important to address several items on the front end. In this chapter, we will determine whether purchasing a commercial property at this time is the right move for you and your business as well as explain the pros and cons of doing so.

Is it wise to purchase a commercial property?

This is the first question I ask my buyer clients during our initial consultation. The prospect of purchasing a piece of commercial property can be extremely exciting for many business owners. It's often a culmination of years of hard work and a strong desire to control their own destiny. However, there are several things to consider prior to beginning your search.

When you buy a commercial building, you're effectively committing to the location for an extended period. Given the fees associated with the sale of real estate (i.e., legal fees, commissions, closing costs etc.), selling within a 5-year window will likely result in you taking a loss on your initial investment.

Second, commercial real estate is illiquid, meaning it's not easily converted into cash. If you fall on hard times and your business requires a cash infusion, it will be difficult to sell your property quickly without taking a significant loss on your investment.

Third, you will need to deploy a sizeable amount of capital to acquire commercial property. Most banks require buyers to come up with between 10-40% of the property value as a down payment for a commercial loan. If you don't have the funds to cover this amount, you won't get very far in the process.

Finally, unlike renting an apartment or a house, there are additional costs associated with owning commercial real estate that business owners often overlook. Below I've provided a list of a few:

1) *Property taxes*
2) *Property insurance*
3) *Regular maintenance of major mechanicals (i.e. HVAC, elevators/escalators, water heater/boiler etc.)*

4) *Large capital expenditures (i.e. replacing roof, HVAC, water heater/boiler etc.)*
5) *As well as many more...*

If you fail to account for these expenses in your initial analysis, you may run into cashflow issues that could put the future of your business in jeopardy.

Therefore, prior to pulling the trigger, it's critical to assess the current and future needs of your business. If you're projecting significant growth, your business is cash strapped, and/or your current cashflow can't justify the additional expenses, it may not be the right time to buy a commercial property.

If this is the case, don't be discouraged. Instead, periodically reassess your needs and, once the time is appropriate, begin your search again. Remember, there is nothing wrong with waiting until you're ready to purchase a commercial property.

The pros and cons of buying commercial property

Now that you've determined you're willing and able to take on the financial responsibility of buying a commercial property, it's important to educate yourself on the acquisition process. Below I've outlined the pros and cons of purchasing commercial real estate and provided feedback on each statement:

Beginning Your Journey

1) **Building equity** – Through a process called *"amortization"*, as you make your monthly mortgage payments, a portion of your loan amount will be paid down. Below, I've provided an infographic that illustrates this concept with a $750,000 commercial loan:

Month	Payment	Principal	Interest	Loan Balance
1	$4,544.85	$2,044.85	$2,500.00	747,955.15
2	$4,544.85	$2,051.67	$2,493.18	745,903.48
3	$4,544.85	$2,058.51	$2,486.34	743,844.97
4	$4,544.85	$2,065.37	$2,479.48	741,779.60
5	$4,544.85	$2,072.25	$2,472.60	739,707.35
6	$4,544.85	$2,079.16	$2,465.69	737,628.19
7	$4,544.85	$2,086.09	$2,458.76	735,542.10
8	$4,544.85	$2,093.05	$2,451.81	733,449.05
9	$4,544.85	$2,100.02	$2,444.83	731,349.03
10	$4,544.85	$2,107.02	$2,437.83	729,242.00
11	$4,544.85	$2,114.05	$2,430.81	727,127.96
12	$4,544.85	$2,121.09	$2,423.76	725,006.87

As you can see, each month that you pay your mortgage, the loan balance is reduced. As a result, you own more and more of your property each month. Over time, this will make a huge impact on your overall net worth.

2) **Tax Advantages** – owning your own building carries a few unique tax advantages:

- According to the Internal Revenue Code (I.R.C), the interest paid on real property mortgage loans, as well as business loans, can be claimed as a deduction. If you itemize your deductions at the end of the year, this will reduce the amount you owe in taxes.

- Your "operating expenses" can also be written off as deductions. Your operating expenses are ones that your business incurs through its normal business operation. For example, maintenance costs, building insurance etc. can be deducted from your gross yearly revenue to reduce your tax liability for the year.

- Owners of commercial real estate can reduce their tax bill by depreciating the value of their property over a set period of time. This shields some of the property's rental income from being taxed, thus, saving you money. For a detailed explanation of the process, check out the link provided here: **https://bit.ly/2UTQiDA**.

3) **Appreciation** – One of the biggest advantages of owning commercial real estate is that, historically, it appreciates over time. For example, if you purchased a well-located commercial property for $1,000,000 today, it will likely be worth more in the future. Along with that, you can force appreciation by making improvements to the building, further increasing its value.

4) **Control** – When you own your building, you don't have to manage a "landlord-tenant" relationship. These relationships can be quite contentious, especially when your lease term expires. In this scenario, you may be forced out of the building if the landlord decides to drastically increase rents or refuses to re-lease the space to you. However, if you own the building, you control your own destiny.

Cons:

1) **Large initial investment** - Purchasing a commercial building will usually require a sizeable down payment. For most commercial loans, banks will want the buyer to allocate between 10-40% of the property value as a down payment. This can be a huge sum, especially if you're just starting out.

2) **Increased maintenance & repair costs** – As the owner of a commercial property, you're responsible for all the regular maintenance & repairs for the building. These items include landscaping, HVAC servicing, painting, interior & exterior modifications etc. In many lease agreements, you're able to pass along some, if not all these expenses to the landlord. This can free up cash you can apply towards growing your business.

3) **Lack of flexibility** – Purchasing a commercial property ties you to a location for an extended period. This is because selling a commercial property, on average, takes much longer than selling a personal residence. If you decide you no longer want to operate your business or you would like to move locations, you'll have to either wait until you're able to sell your property or work with a property manager/commercial agent to move in a new tenant.

Generally, if you plan on occupying a space for a long period of time, you would be wise to consider buying a property to capitalize on equity build-up and appreciation.

However, if you want to maintain flexibility, limit your initial investment, and/or have more working capital available to get your business off the ground, leasing may be your best approach. Since you're reading this book, I'm moving forward under the assumption that you've chosen to purchase a commercial property. Now that you've made your decision, let's talk about the best way to do just that.

> **Pro-tip:** If after reading this section, you believe that leasing commercial space is right for you, check out my book *"Before You Sign That Lease"*. In it, you will learn the step-by-step process to help you lease commercial space as quickly and cost-effectively as possible. To purchase your copy, here is the link: https://amzn.to/3oNt3YX

Action Items

1) Determine if purchasing a piece of commercial property aligns with your business's current and future needs.
   a. If your cashflow can't support it and/or you project significant growth within your business, it may be wise to lease a commercial space instead.
2) Review the pros and cons of purchasing commercial real estate.
   a. Get comfortable with the financial commitment and take some time to plan out future expenditures.

CHAPTER 2
SETTING EXPECTATIONS

"When you align expectation with reality, you will never be disappointed." – **Terrell Owens**

As we highlighted in the previous chapter, the first thing I do when I begin working with a new buyer client is to sit down with them to discuss the pros and cons of purchasing a commercial property. From there, I communicate the realities of the acquisition process and set expectations to prepare them for the road ahead. During this initial consultation, I share 4 main points that my clients must understand prior to beginning their search. To ensure the acquisition process is an enjoyable experience, below I've shared them with you:

There's no such thing as a "perfect property"

Unfortunately, I'm here to be the bearer of bad news. Regardless of your expectations, there's no such thing as the *"perfect"* property. Throughout my career, I've seen small business owners fall victim to this trap time and time again. Many have this fairytale idea of what their business will look like. From the business cards, to the banners, to the layout, to the furniture, to the location and everything in between.

They believe this perfect space is out there and that they will discover it if they look hard enough. Unfortunately, it's often not the case and their lack of success can lead to them becoming disheartened with the entire process.

There will always be something about a property you wish would be different. Whether it's wanting to be located in a more desirable area, sacrificing space due to your budgetary constraints, having an odd interior layout, dealing with deferred maintenance issues etc. Unless you have unlimited resources at your disposal, these pitfalls, as well as many others, will likely arise throughout the course of your search. As a result, work with your commercial real estate agent to adjust your requirements if they don't help you achieve your ultimate objective.

Take some time this week to define your *"must have's"* and *"nice to have's"*. Your must haves are aspects of the space that contribute to the optimal operation of your business. For example, if you own an insurance company with 15 employees, you need a certain amount of space to house them. As a result, a 500 SF office is probably not going to cut it, even if it's in the best location in the world. On the other hand, if you run a manufacturing company that receives several truckloads of supplies each day, having multiple bay doors is a must. Along with that, you may require ceilings of a certain height to move materials within the facility.

If your space doesn't look exactly the way you want it to, don't fret. As we'll learn in the *"Completing Your Build-Out"* chapter of the book, you can work with your general contractor to update the space to meet your unique specifications.

It usually takes longer than you think

This is one of the most common misconceptions I address on the front end of the transaction. Most business owners don't have a frame of reference for how long it takes to purchase commercial real estate. As a result, they often base their assumptions off their experience of buying a home. In most parts of the country, it takes no more than 45 days to purchase a residential property. Although I've helped a few of my clients secure a commercial property within this timeframe, it's definitely not the norm. Usually, the process of identifying, negotiating, inspecting, and occupying a new space takes months to complete. Not only that, but if the space requires renovation, it can add several months to your timeline.

As a result, if you come into the transaction expecting a fast turnaround, you may quickly get disgruntled with the process. To avoid this from happening to you, work with your commercial real estate agent to get crystal clear on your criteria prior to beginning your search. Along with that, if your criteria are too rigid, consider modifying some of the variables to broaden your pool of potential properties. Remember, the more deals you review, the higher the likelihood you have of finding one that aligns with your business goals.

Have your financial documents in order

When you identify a property that you like, the bank will require you to submit financial documents to prove you and/or your business are on solid financial footing. The reason for this is that they want to ensure you're able to comply with the terms of the loan prior to issuing any funds.

Therefore, to expedite the acquisition process, compile the appropriate financial documents and share them with commercial lenders. As we'll highlight later in this book, some of these records may include:

- *Personal Financial Statement*
- *Prior 3 years of Tax Returns*
- *P&L Statement*
- *Balance Sheet*
- *Credit Reports (Personal & Business)*
- *Etc.*

Although this may seem like overkill, I'm of the belief that it's better to be overly prepared than not and thus lose an opportunity.

Your mortgage is not your only expense

Although this may seem like common sense, it's a misconception that continues to persist. I've worked with several business owners who, during our initial consultation, were confident about how much they could afford to spend on their real estate acquisition. However, after considering the many costs associated with owning commercial real estate, they were forced to reevaluate their budget. When you purchase a piece of commercial property, you will not only pay a monthly mortgage payment, but you will also be responsible for a host of other expenses including, but not limited to, property taxes, property insurance, repairs and maintenance, capital reserves, utilities etc. These line items, as well as others, can easily add 10-25% + to your monthly cash outflow! Therefore, work with your commercial real estate agent to estimate these values prior to beginning your search. Some of the actions you can take include:

- *Going to your local property assessor's website to determine tax rates for the area.*
- *Speaking with a commercial insurance agent to get a feel for building and general liability coverage premiums.*
- *Setting aside 3-5% of your yearly operating budget to account for repairs, maintenance, improvements, and other property related expenses.*
- *As well as much more…*

By taking initiative on the front end, you'll save yourself from the heartache and time drain associated with searching for commercial properties outside your price range.

Action Items

1) Understand that there is no such thing as a "perfect" property.
    a. Create a list of "must haves" and "nice to haves".
    b. Work with your commercial real estate agent to identify properties that include the items on your list.
2) Understand that it usually takes longer than you think to purchase a commercial property.
    a. If your criteria is limiting your options, consider modifying them to review more opportunities.
3) Work with your accountant and/or bookkeeper to compile the appropriate financial documentation prior to beginning your search.
    a. In the next chapter, we will identify how to find a stellar accountant who will help you accomplish this goal.
4) Confirm what additional expenses you'll need to account for when creating your final budget.
    a. In the "Determining Your Needs" chapter of the book, we will explore how to incorporate these values into your final budget amount.

CHAPTER 3
ASSEMBLING YOUR REAL ESTATE ADVISORY TEAM

"Great things in business are never done by one person." – **Steve Jobs**

Although you're an expert in your business, you're likely not one in the area of identifying commercial property and negotiating a favorable purchase agreement. For this reason, it's important to surround yourself with a group of stellar individuals who have a fiduciary duty to advocate for your best interests. In this section, we'll discuss how to identify and work with your real estate advisory team to maximize the value you receive from the transaction.

Finding a commercial real estate agent

First, you will want to solicit the services of a competent and effective commercial real estate agent. Since I am one, I'm often met with skepticism when I share this piece of advice. Probably the most common objection I hear is, *"Raphael, why should I work with a commercial real estate agent? Can't I just find a property by myself?"* Although it's not uncommon for business owners to think they can go it alone, I've seen too many suffer adverse consequences, due to their inexperience, to advocate against using one.

First, an experienced commercial real estate agent will have established relationships with owners of commercial properties, other brokers, and reputable service professionals. They can tap into this broad network to help you identify opportunities that meet your criteria.

Second, they're experts in their market and can help you vet the merits of each property. They know the up-and-coming areas, the financial incentives offered by the city, and other location specific information that is invaluable to business owners.

Third, their familiarity with the process will help you avoid the common pitfalls that arise during your due diligence period. They act as the quarterback on the deal and are responsible for ensuring all parties (the buyer, engineers, lawyers etc.) are on the same page and that everyone stays on track to hit the expected deadlines.

Finally, and most importantly, they're 100% FREE for you to use! Generally, the seller is responsible for paying the commission of the brokers involved in the transaction. For this reason, you're able to capitalize on the expertise of your commercial real estate agent without incurring any cost! It's really a no-brainer.

When searching for a stellar commercial real estate agent, you'll want to make sure they have ample experience being a *"buyers' representative"*. A buyer's representative is an agent who focuses solely on the needs of a buyer, rather than being tied to the seller. Here are some of the best strategies you can use to identify a potential candidate:

1) **Searching online** – Probably the easiest way to find a commercial real estate agent is to search for one online. The top agents in town are excellent marketers and will likely have several great reviews praising their ability to close difficult transactions quickly and without major issues.

2) **Asking other business owners** – Many business owners in your area will have worked with a commercial real estate agent to secure their property. If they have a positive experience with one, they will likely refer them to you.

3) **Asking your extended network** – Reach out to your network via LinkedIn, Facebook, Twitter etc. and ask them if they could recommend a commercial real estate agent. Although you'll have to sift through some self-promotional content, you'll likely get solid feedback from other business owners in your area.

4) **Calling signs** – To advertise a property for sale, commercial real estate agents often put-up signs on the premises. Like other professions, the top ones will list the most properties. If you see a lot of the same signs around town, give them a call.

Once you compile a list of potential candidates, interview each one. Some of the questions to consider asking include:

- *What geographic locations do you specialize in?*
- *How long have you been a commercial real estate agent?*
- *Can you tell me about your experience as a buyers' representative?*
- *How many buyers like me have you represented?*
  - *Ask for a list of references.*
- *How will you help me analyze different commercial properties?*
- *Where do you see the market going?*
- *What loan terms are you seeing in the market?*
- *What do I need to prepare before we start the search?*
- *What else should I be asking you?*

Based on their responses, it should be evident whether the agent is a good fit for you. Finally, get clear on how you will communicate with them. Effective communication is the most important component of the real estate transaction. If you and your commercial real estate agent aren't on the same page, it will spell trouble. Therefore, if you prefer to communicate via text and email, make sure they are comfortable using those mediums. If your communication styles don't mesh, it may be wise to move on to another candidate.

Pro-tip: Another common issue I see business owners face is that they decide to use residential agents to help them purchase a commercial property. Although residential agents have good intentions, they're often unaware of the many moving parts involved in a commercial real estate transaction. Because of this, they fall prey to the common obstacles inherent in the due diligence process and their clients ultimately suffer the consequences. Just like you wouldn't hire a plastic surgeon to perform a heart operation, you shouldn't ask a residential agent to handle your commercial transaction.

Finding a real estate lawyer

This is one member of your team you do not want to skimp on. A real estate lawyer is someone whose job it is to know the rules and regulations related to real estate transactions. They help their clients understand real estate contracts and other legal documents. It's critical that you find an attorney who has a lot of experience working on commercial transactions. Given their expertise, they will help you avoid potentially catastrophic pitfalls that could put you at risk legally.

To find a stellar real estate attorney, start by asking your commercial real estate agent. They deal with commercial transactions daily and will likely know a few great lawyers to recommend. Along with that, ask other business owners within your network. If they own their commercial property and had a pleasant experience with their real estate attorney, they will likely vouch for them. Once you have a list of potential candidates, interview each one. Some of the questions to consider asking include:

- *Are you primarily a real estate lawyer?*
  - *If not, how much of your business is geared toward property and contract law?*
- *How long have you been practicing real estate law?*
- *How many commercial transactions have you handled?*
- *How does your billing work?*
- *How much will your services cost?*
- *Will I be working with you or someone else?*
  - *If someone else, how much experience do they have working in real estate law?*
- *Do you have references?*
- *What else should I be asking you?*

Like your commercial real estate agent, get clear on how you will communicate with them. Effective communication is the most important component of a real estate transaction. If you and your real estate attorney aren't on the same page, it will spell trouble. Therefore, if you prefer to communicate with text and email, make sure they're comfortable using those mediums. If your communication styles don't mesh, it may be wise to move on to another candidate.

Finally, make sure they are a *"deal maker"* and not a *"deal breaker"*. What I mean by this is that some attorneys are masters at identifying problems with every action you propose. However, they don't offer any creative solutions that will help you achieve your ultimate objective while protecting your legal interests. On the other hand, stellar real estate lawyers are ones who provide alternative strategies that achieve the same or similar objectives while protecting you legally. If you plan on associating with an attorney, make sure they're the deal making kind.

Finding an accountant

These professionals are worth their weight in gold. During the acquisition process, you will likely be asked to furnish various financial documents. This is because your commercial lender will want to verify that you're able to take on the financial obligation of owning a piece of commercial property. Your accountant will work with you to compile these documents as well as ensure that the information presented is accurate. Below I've provided examples of financial documents your commercial lender may request:

1) **Personal Financial Statements** - *A disclosure of your assets, liabilities, annual income, and annual expenditures.*

2) **Tax Returns** - *Documents filed with a tax authority that report your income, expenses, and other relevant financial information to assess your tax obligation.*

3) **Profit and Loss statements** – *A financial document that shows the revenues and expenses of you or your company during a particular period.*

4) **Balance Sheets** – A summary of the financial balances of you or your organization.

5) **Credit reports** - A record of a borrower's responsible repayment of debts.

Probably the best way to identify a great business accountant is by asking fellow business owners in your area. Most business owners use an accountant and will likely recommend one if they have a great working relationship. Along with that, consider asking your extended network via LinkedIn, Facebook, Twitter etc. Once you identify a few candidates, interview each one. Some of the questions to consider asking include:

- *How long have you been in business?*
- *How many businesses like me have you worked with?*
  a. *Do you have references?*
- *What services do you provide?*
- *Can you represent me in all the states I do business?*
- *Will I be working with you or someone else?*
  - *If someone else, how much experience do they have working as an accountant?*
- *Are you available year-round?*
  - *Some accounting firms shut their doors after April 15th and reopen for the following tax season.*
- *How often will we meet to discuss my business taxes?*
- *What else should I be asking you?*

Like your commercial real estate agent and real estate attorney, get clear on how you will communicate with them. If you prefer to communicate via text and email, make sure they're comfortable using those mediums as well. If your communication styles don't mesh, it may be wise to move on to another candidate. Remember, your relationship with your accountant will survive long after you purchase your new commercial property. As a result, you want to make sure you select someone who's competent, responsive and has values that align with yours.

Finding a commercial general contractor

Although a commercial space may be move-in ready, it's not always the case. Sometimes, the property's current configuration is sub-optimal, additional functionality is required, or the prior owners use was completely unrelated to yours. In these instances, you'll need to solicit the services of a licensed commercial general contractor.

A commercial general contractor (GC) is a professional who is responsible for the day-to-day oversight of a construction site, management of vendors and trades, and the communication of information to all involved parties throughout the course of a commercial building project. Hiring a reputable and competent GC takes the pressure of managing a construction project off you so you can focus on getting your business up and running.

Since GC's charge a fee for their services, many of my cost-conscious clients ask, *"Why should I hire a GC if I can contract out the work myself and save money?"*. Renovating commercial space can be a laborious and stressful process. As an example, if you're looking to convert a retail space into a functional restaurant in Louisville, KY, here are just some of the items you'll need to address:

- *Installing a 3 – compartment sink.*
- *Installing hand sink(s) that are accessible to workstations.*
- *Ensuring there is hot and cold water with sufficient pressure.*
- *Installing a waste-tank that's 50% or larger than your freshwater tank.*
- *Installing refrigeration unit (s) that register temperatures of 41°F or below.*
- *Fitting the space with the proper electrical wiring to ensure your equipment functions as intended.*
- *Adding or tearing down walls to create a functional layout.*
- *Installing proper ventilation to ensure hot air is escaping the kitchen correctly.*
- *As well as many more…*

For this job alone, you would need to hire electricians, plumbers, drywall contractors, concrete contractors, roofers etc. Coordinating all these individuals and ensuring the work is done properly and on time can be a stressful and cumbersome experience. Instead of focusing your efforts in this area, you would be better served addressing other business-related items to ensure you're ready to begin operations once construction is complete.

Choosing your general contractor

Now that you understand the value of hiring a stellar GC, it's time to identify potential GC candidates. To start, ask your commercial real estate agent if they know anyone they would recommend. Your agent will likely have worked with multiple commercial contractors in the past and will be happy to provide you with a list of vetted professionals. Along with that, ask other business owners in your social sphere if they know of any good commercial contractors. Like you, many business owners have used commercial contractors in the past to modify their existing space. If they had a good experience with one, they will likely recommend them to you. Finally, search online to find the best rated ones in your area. When reading their reviews, look for references to the quality of their work, their responsiveness, timeliness, and ability to stay on budget. These characteristics, along with many others, are ones that all great commercial contractors possess.

It's important to note that you need to verify that each contractor is licensed and bonded in the state where the work will be performed. Although individuals who aren't may offer a better price, it's often not worth the risk. Licensed general contractors are held to a high ethical standard and are required to maintain insurance policies that cover them if any legal actions are taken against them. As a result, it will be much easier to collect damages if issues arise during the project and you're forced to file a complaint. Once you've compiled a list of at least 5 potential candidates, interview each one. Some of the questions to consider asking include:

1) Do you have prior experience with these types of projects?
2) How do you manage your scheduling?
3) Can you give me a timeline for the work that needs to be done?
4) Will you be my contact person on this project?
    a. If not, does my contact have experience with similar projects?
5) How do you handle site supervision?
6) How much will I need to put down?
a. If the contractor wants more than half the money up front, be wary. Most reputable contractors will likely only request enough to cover the initial material costs for the job.
7) What else should I be asking you?

Like the other professionals you hired, get clear on how you will communicate with them as well as the frequency with which you will do so. Renovating a commercial space is an in-depth process that requires constant communication between you and your GC. If you prefer to communicate via text and email, make sure they're comfortable using those mediums as well. After interviewing each one, select your top 3 candidates.

Pro-tip: Like the rest of your real estate advisory team, it's important to verify that your general contractor has experience completing commercial construction projects. Although residential GC's can perform the work, they're often unaware of the many nuances associated with building out a commercial space. This increases the chances of an error occurring which will cost you time and money to remedy. Along with that, they likely won't have established relationships with the appropriate sub-contractors who will help bring the project to a successful completion. Just like you wouldn't hire an auto mechanic to fix a jet engine, don't hire a residential contractor to perform a commercial buildout.

Action Items

1) Compile a list of the top commercial real estate agents in your area.
    a. Schedule appointments to interview them and select the one that meets your criteria.
2) Ask your commercial real estate agent and your network to recommend a great real estate attorney.
    a. Once you identify a few, interview each one and select the lawyer with the best track record of success.
    b. Make sure they are a "deal maker" and not a "deal breaker".
3) Ask fellow business owners and your extended network to recommend a great accountant.
    a. Interview them and select the one who's values align with your and those of your business.
    b. Work with them to compile the financial documents you will need to secure a commercial loan.
4) Ask your commercial real estate agent to recommend several commercial general contractors.
    a) Come up with a list of at least 5 and interview each one.
    b) Narrow down your list to your top 3 candidates.

CHAPTER 4
IDENTIFYING COMMERCIAL LENDERS

"When looking for funding, don't just look for cash. Look for the right people." – **Jodie Fox**

Now that you have your all-star real estate advisory team in place, let's discuss how to secure commercial financing. Although there are a variety of institutions that lend on commercial real estate (i.e., Life Insurance Companies, CMBS, Debt Funds, Government Sponsored Entities etc.), this chapter will focus on securing a commercial loan through a local or national bank. Unlike residential real estate, commercial lenders are much less common, and most are quite particular about the properties they choose to lend on. Therefore, in this section we will explain how to find commercial lenders who will be a great partner to work with.

> **Disclaimer:** To be clear, I am not a commercial lender. All the information shared in this section is based on my own independent research, my personal experience, the experiences of my clients as well as conversations I've had with professionals within the banking industry. If you have any questions and/or concerns with any topic discussed in this section, please seek the advice of an experienced commercial banker.

Finding commercial banks

To start, you will need to compile a list of several commercial banks in your area. This can be somewhat challenging as not all banks offer commercial loans. Not only that, but of those that do, some may prefer to lend on particular property types. For example, some may have an appetite for owner occupied retail stores and investment properties while others may not. Some may love to loan on self-storage and multifamily properties while others prefer hotels and ground up developments.

The current economic climate will also dictate how willing banks are to loan money. In times of economic prosperity, commercial lenders loosen their lending criteria and capital flows more freely. However, during economic recessions, banks tighten their purse strings and buyers who would previously qualify for a loan may find themselves unable to do so.

Given the multitude of variables involved with choosing the best bank to partner with, it's crucial that you speak with as many commercial lenders as you can. Here are some of the best ways to identify them:

1) **Asking your commercial real estate agent** – *This is probably the most effective strategy. Commercial real estate agents interact with commercial banks on a regular basis. As a result, they usually have a solid understanding of terms offered by various lenders in town as well as*

their preference for business uses. As a result, they can recommend those that align well with your objective and, thus, can help streamline the process of qualifying for financing.

2) **Searching online** – Another great way to find commercial banks in your area is to search for them online. Utilize keywords such as "business lending", "SBA", "commercial loans" etc. Along with that, look for portfolios of projects they have funded over the years. Some local commercial lenders will have a page dedicated to these projects on their website.

3) **Attending Chamber of Commerce events** – One of the best places to find commercial bankers is at your local Chamber of Commerce events. Commercial bankers love attending these functions because they get to interact with their target clients, business owners. Therefore, by regularly attending these gatherings, you'll meet a variety of lenders who are eager to discuss their latest loan offerings.

4) **Asking other business owners** –Business owners who own commercial property will likely have worked with a commercial banker in the past. If they're located in your area, consider asking them for a recommendation. If they've had a positive experience with one, they will likely refer them to you.

Once you compile a list of 5-7 lenders, reach out to each one and explain your objective. Ask them to provide you with a list of all the information and documents they will need from you to qualify for commercial financing. These items may include, but are not limited to:

- *Business and Personal Tax Returns*
- *Your books, records, and financial reports.*
- *Last three months or more of bank statements.*
- *Details regarding collateral (i.e., balance sheet)*
- *Business plan (if it's a start up).*

Once you have this list, work with your commercial real estate advisory team to compile the appropriate documents and submit them to each lender. Although you likely won't receive a definitive *"pre-approval"* without a signed purchase agreement in place, they will often give you a ballpark figure of what you will likely qualify for.

Finally, ask each one how long it will take them to fund the loan after you're approved. Some banks take longer than others, so you want to ensure you request enough time within your final purchase contract to secure the loan.

> **Pro-tip:** From my own personal experience, local lenders tend to offer the most competitive terms and are more flexible than national lenders. Since local banks have less overhead, they're able to pass along these savings to their customers. Not only that, but because many are headquartered locally, they have a deep-rooted understanding of the market and, thus, will often be more comfortable issuing loans. Finally, they're typically more responsive and willing to work

> with you throughout the lending process. If it's your first go around, I would highly recommend leaning towards using a local lender.

Should I seek SBA Financing?

This is a question I often get asked when I begin working with my business owner clients. The Small Business Administration (S.B.A) is a United States Government Agency that provides support to entrepreneurs and small business owners by offering competitive loans, grants, and other incentives. Contrary to popular belief, the SBA does not issue loans to business owners. They guarantee a portion of the loan issued by lending institutions, thus, lowering their risk in the deal. The SBA program has the following offerings:

- *7(a) loan* – *This is SBA's flagship product. Borrowers can secure general financing of up to $5 million to cover most business purposes, such as working capital, fixed assets and purchasing real estate. For more information on this loan product, check out the following link:*

  https://www.sba.gov/funding-programs/loans/7a-loans

- *504 loan* – *This loan provides long-term, fixed rate financing of up to $5 million for major fixed assets that promote business growth and job creation. These include the purchase and construction of existing buildings or land, new facilities, long-term machinery, and equipment as well as the improvement or modernization of land, streets, utilities, parking lots and landscaping and existing* facilities. *These funds cannot be used for working capital. For more information on this loan product, check out the following link:*

https://www.sba.gov/funding-programs/loans/504-loans

Typically, business owners interested in acquiring commercial real estate elect to go with the 504-loan program. This is because the 504 loan offers lower down payment requirements, longer amortization periods, and the ability to fix your interest rate over the life of the loan. These loan characteristics make it easier to predict what your mortgage payment will be in the future, thus, stabilizing your business's cashflow over time.

In my practice, I often sit down with my clients to review the pros and cons of the SBA loan program to determine whether it's wise for them to pursue. Below I've highlighted a few of the most important:

Pros:

1) **Lower Down Payment** – This is probably the most often cited reason why business owners pursue SBA financing. Unlike conventional banks that require 20-40% down payments, the SBA has down payment requirements as low as 10%. Depending on the size of your loan, this modification can save you tens, if not hundreds of thousands of dollars in capital that you can instead deploy within your business.

2) **Longer Amortization Periods** – Typically, commercial lenders offer amortization periods ranging from 10-20 years. However, the SBA 504 loan offers amortization periods of up to 25 years! This means your loan payments are spread over a longer period which reduces your monthly mortgage payment.

3) **Ability to fund other business expenses** – Depending on which loan option you choose, you may be able to fund other business expenses such as working capital, inventory, machinery and even the acquisition of another business.

Cons:

1) **SBA Fee** – This is probably the most common complaint I hear about SBA financing. The SBA fee is an amount charged by the SBA to keep the program going for future business owner applicants. It ranges from 2 - 3.75% of the loan amount depending on its size and the percentage that is guaranteed by the SBA. If you're planning to take out a sizable loan, this fee could equate to tens of thousands of dollars.

2) **Slow Process** – The SBA is notoriously slow at processing loan requests. When seeking conventional financing, it usually takes between 30-60 days to process a loan. With the SBA, 90-day processing times are not uncommon, and some take even longer. If you plan to seek SBA financing, let your commercial real estate

agent know so they can specify your intent in the final purchase contract.

3) **Requires a personal guarantee** – This can be a turn off to some business owners. Prior to securing a SBA loan, the agency will require you to personally guarantee the note. This means that if your business were to default on the loan, the agency could come after your personal assets.

As a general rule, if you place a premium on having the lowest possible mortgage payment, you're in an industry where its critical to retain large capital reserves, and/or you would like to finance other business-related expenses (i.e., working capital, inventory, machinery, etc.) it may be wise to consider seeking SBA financing. However, if you can qualify for conventional financing and the mortgage payment is easily affordable, I would encourage you to pursue the conventional route. Although there are some hoops you'll have to jump through, securing SBA financing can be a powerful tool for small business owners.

> **Pro-tip:** If you do decide to seek SBA financing, use a bank that is an *"SBA Preferred Lender"*. This designation signifies that a bank has the authority to make final credit decisions on SBA-guaranteed loans. By contrast, non-preferred lenders must submit loan applications directly to the SBA for approval, which drags out the process. SBA preferred lenders also fund a significant amount of SBA loans so they can provide constructive feedback on your loan package to improve your chances of qualifying.

Action Items

1) *Employ the strategies discussed in this chapter to create a list of 5-7 commercial lenders.*
2) *Work with your real estate advisory team to compile the documents requested by each lending institution.*
3) *Determine whether pursuing a SBA loan is right for you.*
   a. *Remember, if having a lower down payment, money for working capital and/or a lower mortgage payment is important to you, it may be wise to explore SBA Financing.*

CHAPTER 5
DETERMINING YOUR NEEDS

"Understanding the needs of your business is the starting point for any project." – **John Williams**

Before beginning your search, you must first get clear on what your current needs are. It doesn't make sense to start looking for commercial properties prior to knowing exactly what your business requires and what you can afford. In this section, we will seek to define the following criteria: your budget, size requirements and desired location.

Budget

This is probably the most important variable to consider prior to beginning your search as it's often the least flexible. Your upper limit purchase price will depend on a variety of factors including your total down payment, interest rate, amortization period, term length etc. We will explore how banks determine this value in the *"Working with your Lender"* chapter of the book. However, the variables that will most impact your business's bottom line will be your down payment and monthly mortgage payment.

Most commercial banks have down payment requirements ranging from 20-40% of the total purchase price. If you seek out a SBA loan, the down payment requirements can be as low as 10%. You may currently have enough in the bank to cover your down payment. However, just because you have the funds, does not mean you should allocate everything you have. Regardless of how diligent you are when assessing the condition of a commercial property, something unexpected almost always comes up. Therefore, I often recommend my client's set aside reserve funds to account for any issues that may arise after closing. These items may include:

1) *Replacing/Repairing mechanicals*
2) *Renovations of the existing space*
3) *Addressing deferred maintenance items*
4) *Updating fixtures*
5) *Reorganizing landscaping*
6) *As well as much more....*

As a rule of thumb, I recommend setting aside between 4-6 months of recurring property expenses in reserves prior to closing. This means that if a property costs $5,000 to operate each month (i.e., mortgage payment, taxes, insurance, repair & maintenance etc.), you should set aside between $20,000-$30,000 in reserves. This will create a buffer to help you deal with any unexpected expenses that arise after closing. Take some time this week to determine how much you're comfortable allocating towards a down payment. Once you have this number in mind, the next variable to consider is how much your business can afford to pay as a monthly mortgage payment.

Now you may be thinking, *"I have no idea how much I can afford to pay each month!"*. To calculate this value, I encourage my clients to use a metric called, "Debt-to-Income Ratio" (DTI). In this context, your DTI is the percentage of your business's gross income that goes towards paying debts. This value is calculated using the following equation:

$$DTI = \frac{\text{Monthly Debt Obligations}}{\text{Monthly Gross Income}}$$

Where your monthly gross income is your business's gross revenue minus its cost of goods sold (COGS) and your monthly debt obligations include the summation of all monthly debt payments including your mortgage, expenses for real estate taxes, building insurance premiums, car payments, business credit card payments, equipment payments etc. To better understand this point, let's imagine that you operate a business with the following performance metrics:

Yearly Gross Revenue = $660,000
COGS = $300,000

Based on these values, your business's yearly gross income would be $360,000 ($30,000 per month). If your recurring monthly payments for equipment, vehicles, lines of credit, etc. equals $5,000 per month, your current DTI ratio would be as follows:

$$\$5,000/\$30,000 = 16.66\%$$

After having conversations with several lenders, you determine your DTI ratio cannot exceed 50%. Therefore, your maximum monthly mortgage payment would be as follows:

$$\frac{(\text{Monthly Mortgage Payment} + \$5000)}{\$30,000} = 50\%$$

Monthly Mortgage Payment + $5,000 = $15,000

Monthly Mortgage Payment = $10,000

As you can see, your lender will likely determine that your monthly mortgage payment, including property taxes and insurance, should not exceed $10,000. Having said that, just because your business can support this amount, does not necessarily mean it should. Every business owner must determine what they're comfortable paying. Therefore, if after reviewing the numbers you feel uneasy, lower the mortgage payment until you're satisfied.

Once you have these numbers in hand, share them with your commercial lender. These data points, along with your personal and business financial documents, will help your lender determine the appropriate loan amount for your business. Once they calculate your final loan amount, update your commercial real estate agent. They will use this metric to modify your search criteria so you can identify properties that align with your budgetary requirements.

Size

The second item to consider is how much space you will need to operate your business. In commercial real estate, the metric most often used to describe this requirement is your total *"square footage"* (SF). Like your budget, size requirements will vary widely depending on your use. For example, if you run a manufacturing business, you may need to purchase a large warehouse with high ceilings and plenty of open space to operate heavy machinery, store raw materials, as well as a host of other functions.

On the other hand, if you're looking to purchase an office building, your space requirement will be completely different. In this scenario, a good rule of thumb would be to factor in between 125–200 SF per person. This range accounts for a 10x12 foot office per person plus additional space for waiting rooms, walkways, reception areas etc. As a result, if you're running a 10-person operation, your space requirement will likely be anywhere between 1,250–2,500 SF.

If you own a retail business, your space requirement will be dependent on what goods/services you're selling, how much inventory you need to store, how many employees you have etc. For example, grocers usually require much more open space than service businesses such as barbers, nail salons, chiropractors etc. Along with that, restaurants need to have dedicated space for a dining area as well as room for a kitchen. The space must also comply with city codes and regulations to ensure the proper and safe operation of the restaurant.

Finally, consider the expansion capabilities of the property. When you purchase a commercial building, you're committing to the space for an extended period, often 5 years or more. If you don't account for future growth, you may run out of room sooner than expected.

Therefore, if your business projects explosive growth, it may be wise to consider properties that have extra land to build on or a property that has a larger footprint than you currently desire. That way, you maintain flexibility and limit the downside risk of outgrowing your space.

Location

You've probably heard the saying that real estate is all about *"location, location, location"*. However, the ideal location for one business owner will not be the same for another. For example, if you're a retailer, occupying a space that has great visibility along major roadways will be of value to you. As a result, you may elect to purchase or construct a property along a road with high traffic counts, great visibility, and accessibility.

If you want to open an insurance office, you may not care how visible the property is. Because of this, you may opt to buy a building with a larger footprint in a more remote location with ample parking. At the other end of the spectrum, if you operate a manufacturing business, being close to your primary suppliers and having easy access to major roadways will be critical. Because of this variability, you need to get clear on your business goals and define how each of these requirements will help you achieve your objectives. Some of the questions to consider include:

- *Is the property located in an area suitable for your use?*
    - *Is it near offices, homes, other businesses?*
- *Is it close to interstates and/or roads with high traffic counts?*
- *How easy is it to drive to the property?*
    - *Is there a dedicated turn lane to enter and exit?*
    - *Can you access it from a major roadway, or do you have to turn onto a side street?*
- *If you're a retailer, service professional and/or restaurateur:*
    - *Are potential customers able to see your establishment?*
    - *Is it tucked away behind other buildings and/or another major retail center?*
    - *Do you have signs on the premises you can utilize?*

Your commercial real estate agent should help you answer these questions as well as provide you with the data you'll need to make an informed decision on each property.

Action Items

1) Determine how much you can afford to spend each month on your down payment and monthly mortgage payment.
2) Get clear on how much space you'll need to operate your business.
    a. Ensure it's functional for your use.
    b. Will you need storage, a commercial kitchen, bay doors etc.?
    c. Will you outgrow the space within the next 5-7 years?
3) Analyze where the best location for your business would be.
    a. Consider why being located in that area will help your business grow.
    b. Are you giving up something of significance to be in that location?

CHAPTER 6
FINDING YOUR NEW PROPERTY

"There wouldn't be a sky full of stars if we were all meant to wish on the same one." – **Frances Clark**

Now that you're clear on your criteria, the fun is about to begin! Going forward, you will work with your commercial real estate agent to find a property that fits your unique business needs. In this chapter, we will highlight how to identify opportunities, assess their viability, and determine market values for commercial properties.

Identifying potential properties

The first step is to identify properties that fulfill the needs of your business. Review properties online via your local commercial real estate listing platform as well as national sites such as Crexi and LoopNet. Have your commercial real estate agent set you up on a weekly email drip campaign that sends you listings that meet your criteria.

Second, consider driving around town and looking for signs that read, *"for sale".* If you find a space that you like, provide the contact information to your commercial real estate agent and have them call the owner on your behalf.

Third, stop by your local chamber of commerce and inquire about available properties in your area. Often, they will have a directory of properties available for sale. If you're a chamber member and you're willing to get your hands dirty (i.e., renovate an existing structure), they may be willing to offer you a property at a favorable purchase price.

Finally, reach out to your network via LinkedIn, Facebook, Instagram etc. and express your interest in buying a commercial property. Provide your criteria and timeline for wanting to move in. If your network is broad and diverse enough, you may have a connection or two who can point you in the right direction.

Reviewing your options

Once you and your commercial real estate agent compile a list of potential properties, set up appointments to view each one. If possible, schedule them on the same day or as close together as possible. This will ensure your memory is fresh so you can effectively compare them prior to making your final decision. As you tour each space, take pictures, and write detailed notes on what you see.

Whenever I tour a property, I organize the corresponding photos and notes in a folder on my google drive for easy access later. If the interior needs work, consider asking one of your top 3 contractors to walk the property with you. They will give you a better idea of what it will cost to make the interior functional for your use.

After completing the tours, sit down with your commercial real estate agent to discuss the pros and cons of each. Reference your *"must haves"* and *"nice to haves"* as well as your budget, size and location requirements. When I perform this analysis with my clients, we grade each from first to last based on how in-line they are with their criteria.

> **Pro-tip:** When reviewing potential opportunities, ensure that each is properly zoned to allow for your business use. Zoning laws dictate what businesses can locate at a particular site. Therefore, if a property is zoned for a general retail use, you likely won't be able to open a jet engine manufacturing plant. Each municipality has its own zoning laws and likely its own vernacular to describe different types of zoning. Therefore, reference your city's land development code to confirm. You can typically access this document via an online search or by heading to the offices of your local zoning board.

Determining commercial property values

After reviewing your options, you must determine an appropriate offer price for your top choice. Contrary to popular belief, a property's asking price may not always be in-line with its actual value. Therefore, it's important to perform your own independent analysis to determine an appropriate offer price.

Since you're purchasing the property as an owner occupant (i.e., you will be operating your business out of the building), commercial appraisers will utilize a valuation method called the *"comparable approach"* to determine the final property value. This method compares the *"subject property"* (i.e., your building) to others with similar characteristics that have recently sold in the area. Once comparisons are made, you can approximate a *"price per square foot"* range and use that to determine what the subject property may be worth.

To start, your commercial real estate agent will research similar properties that have recently sold. Depending on the volume of transactions within your market, they may need to go back several years to compile a list. Once they complete this step, they will compare the unique characteristics of each property to the subject property. Some of these characteristics include:

- *Total Square Feet*
- *Geographic location*
- *Age*
- *Size*
- *Condition*
- *Acreage*
- *Zoning*
- *As well as much more…*

A greater weight will be placed on properties that have sold recently and those that are most like the subject property. After completing their analysis, your commercial real estate agent will specify a *"price per square foot"* range as an approximation of its market value. To better illustrate this point, I've provided an example below:

Let's imagine you're interested in making an offer on a 30,000 SF industrial building with 2 dock doors and several drive-in bays. Your commercial real estate agent performs a market analysis and determines recent comparable properties have sold for between $120-$130 per square foot (PSF). To determine the property's market value, use the following equation:

> *Property Value=*
> *Total Square Feet * Price Per Square Foot*

Given these variables, the approximate value of the subject property would be as follows:

> *Property Value (Low)=30,000 SF* $120 PSF*
> *Property Value (High)=30,000 SF* $130 PSF*
> *Property Value (Range)=$3,600,000-$3,900,000*

Therefore, the market value of the subject property is likely within this range. Having said that, it may be slightly more or less depending on its condition and other inherent characteristics of the property (i.e., location, amenities etc.). As you can see, this is certainly not an exact science. However, by performing this analysis, you'll get a better feel for what market rates are and, thus, can make an informed decision on a fair offer price.

Pro-tip: For a detailed analysis on one that I conducted recently, check out the following link:
https://bit.ly/3IdEUbQ

Action Items

1) Employ the strategies discussed in this section to identify available properties that meet your criteria.
2) Tour each space and take pictures and detailed notes.
   a. If the space needs work, bring a general contractor along to provide insight on the build out that will be required.
3) Once you complete your viewings, sit down with your commercial real estate agent to narrow down your list.
   a. Reference your "must haves" and "nice to haves" list as well as your budget, location and space requirements.
4) Perform a comparable market analysis on your top choices to determine an appropriate value for each one.
   a. Work with your commercial real estate agent to compile a list of recent sales.

CHAPTER 7
DRAFTING YOUR PURCHASE AGREEMENT

"It's impossible to unsign a contract, so do all your thinking before you sign." – **Warren Buffett**

You've reached a significant milestone in the acquisition process! Now that you've performed a detailed analysis on your top choice, you're ready to draft the purchase and sale agreement. In this chapter we will highlight some of the most important provisions within a commercial purchase contract and provide insights on how to make your offer as compelling as possible.

> **Disclaimer:** To be clear, I am not a lawyer, nor do I claim to be. The information provided in this section has been compiled based on my own personal experience, the experience of my clients and conversations I've had with legal professionals. If you have any questions and/or concerns regarding any of the content contained in this chapter, please seek the advice of a licensed real estate attorney.

Property Description

The first part of your offer should include a property description. A property description is one that clearly defines the real estate that is being acquired. Basic details about the property may include:

- *Full Property Address*
- *City, State & Zip code*
- *Acreage*
- *Square Footage*
- *Parcel ID (if applicable)*
- *As well as much more...*

To verify the property description, go to your local property assessor's official website and search their online records. In Louisville, KY our local assessor is called the "Property Valuation Administration" (P.V.A). However, it may be called something different in your state. If your municipality or jurisdiction charges a fee to access property information, ask your commercial real estate agent to execute the search for you. Since they operate in the market, they will likely subscribe to their software. For examples of what a property description looks like, speak with your real estate attorney.

> **Pro-tip:** To be clear, the property lines specified in the property assessor's records are not always 100% accurate. That's why I highly recommend commissioning a survey when purchasing commercial real estate. This

report will detail exactly what you're buying and if any easements, encroachments etc. exist. In the *"Performing a Survey"* section of the book, we'll explain the importance of securing one and how it can help you avoid catastrophic consequences after your purchase.

Purchase Price

This will likely be the most hotly contested item during contract negotiations. I've been involved in many transactions where the purchase price is the sole item of contention. All the rest of the contract provisions were secondary, even though they carried significant weight. Through my experience, I have found that to achieve the most favorable purchase price, you must put yourself in the seller's shoes.

Sellers want to work with buyers who can execute on the transaction. They don't want to tie up their property for months only to have it fall through at the 11th hour. When this happens, they lose momentum, and it will likely be harder to achieve an optimal sales price the next time around. Additionally, many don't want to deal with repairing and/or modifying the property prior to a sale. Therefore, if you can prove to the seller that you can close and you're open to taking the property *"as-is"*, they're more likely to accept a reduced offer. Additional suggestions include shortening your due diligence, financing, and closing timeline.

Having said that, there are instances where, despite your best efforts, the seller is not receptive. If you find yourself at an impasse, you must consider whether the opportunity is worth pursuing. However, prior to making your final decision, consider the *"opportunity cost"* of waiting. Opportunity cost is defined as the loss of potential gain from other alternatives when one path is chosen. Essentially, you want to ask yourself, *"how much will walking away from this opportunity cost my business?"*

I've worked on several transactions where my clients failed to consider these alternative scenarios. In one instance, my client nearly walked away from a $2.6 million dollar deal over a $10,000 difference in purchase price. That's 0.4% of the entire transaction! Not only that, but $10,000 financed with a commercial loan at 4% with a 25-year amortization period would have equated to $44.47 per month in additional mortgage payments.

If he had walked away from the opportunity, how would it have impacted his business? To start, he would have likely waited months, if not years, for another property with similar characteristics to come along. In the meantime, he would have had hiring constraints due to the size of their current location and a limited capacity for additional inventory, thus, resulting in a lower sales volume. After analyzing the alternative, it's easy to see that the opportunity cost of refusing the seller's counteroffer would have been WAY more than $10,000. As a result, walking away would not have been a wise business decision.

Understand that this item is not the end all be all. You may still be able to work out a favorable deal by conceding some on the purchase price in exchange for adjustments to other provisions within the purchase contract. We'll discuss these items, as well as many more, throughout the rest of this chapter.

Earnest money deposit

The next step in the process is to specify what you're willing to put up as an *"earnest money deposit"*. Earnest money, or a good faith deposit, is a sum of money you put down to demonstrate your seriousness about buying a property. This amount will be credited towards your down payment when you close on the property.

If you release the contract during your due diligence period, the earnest money deposit will be refunded to you. On the other hand, if you attempt to back out after your due diligence period has expired, you will forfeit your deposit to the Seller. Because of this, it's extremely important to document and set reminders for key contingency deadlines within the contract.

To make your offer more enticing to the Seller, putting up a larger earnest money deposit may be an effective approach. Typically, the larger the amount, the more serious you are perceived to be. Additionally, making part or all the deposit *"non-refundable"* can be extremely enticing to the seller. In a very competitive market, this strategy can put you over the top when compared to competing offers.

Contingencies

When you submit a purchase offer, it's important to ensure that you have *"contingencies"* in place to give you flexibility. Contingencies are clauses within a real estate purchase agreement specifying an action or requirement that must be met so that the contract can become legally binding. Buyers typically include contingencies within a contract to mitigate the impact of unforeseen circumstances on their decision to purchase the property. Although there are an infinite number of contingencies that can be created, the most common are:

> ***Inspection Contingency*** *– This provision gives you the right to inspect the property to determine its condition. If during your inspection period, you uncover information that makes the property no longer attractive to purchase, you may back out of your contract without forfeiting your earnest money deposit. This period usually ranges anywhere between 30-90 days.*
>
> ***Financing contingency*** *– This provision specifies the financing terms you will be seeking from your desired lending institution. If you're unable to secure financing or you're unable to achieve your desired loan terms, you have the right to back out of the contract without forfeiting your earnest money deposit. This period usually ranges anywhere between 30-90 days.*

Environmental contingency – *This provision conditions the closing of the sale on a satisfactory report on the environmental conditions affecting the property. Therefore, if after reviewing the property's environmental report you deem it unsatisfactory, you can back out of the contract without forfeiting your earnest money deposit. This contingency is especially important for properties that are believed to have environmental contamination (i.e., dry cleaner, gas stations, factories, etc.) This period usually ranges anywhere between 30-90 days.*

Rezoning contingency – *This provision is critical if the property is not currently zoned to fit your intended use. The rezoning process can take months or even years to complete. Therefore, to limit your risk, this contingency gives you the right to back out of the contract without forfeiting your earnest money deposit if you don't achieve your desired zoning. This period usually ranges anywhere between 90-180 days and sometimes even longer depending on how contentious the rezoning is predicted to be. The rezoning process is not for the faint of heart and should only be undertaken if you feel confident in your chances and you have a stellar zoning attorney, engineer & architect in your corner.*

Sellers usually prefer offers with as few contingencies as possible. This is because contingencies enable a potential buyer to back out of the contract with limited to no consequences. When a property falls out of contract, there is typically a negative stigma attached to it. As a result, momentum is lost, and the final sale price can be negatively impacted.

Therefore, if you want to increase the competitiveness of your offer, you may consider shortening your contingency timeframes and/or eliminating them altogether. Having said that, I believe this strategy should only be pursued by those who have a significant amount of experience acquiring commercial property. I do not recommend that you pursue this route if you're a first-time buyer.

> **Pro-tip:** Prior to setting your contingency dates, make sure you have a clear understanding of how long it will take to complete each one. In the past, I've been involved in transactions with several agents who underestimated the time it would take them to complete certain items. As a result, they were forced to ask for extension after extension which greatly frustrated all involved and put the deal in jeopardy. To start, ask your commercial lender how long it will take them to complete the loan for the property. Additionally, confirm inspection timelines with your commercial inspector and/or individual trades people who will be assessing the physical condition of the building.

Extension Options

In instances where finalizing your due diligence process may extend farther than your contract allows, it may be wise to include an *"Extension Option"* within the original agreement. An extension option is one that allows you to extend your due diligence period if certain conditions are met. This extension can be automatic (i.e., extended after the deadline even if no written notice is given) or can require written notice be given to the seller.

I've only seen these provisions used when a buyer wishes to purchase a property that will need to be rezoned. Since the rezoning process can take many months and sometimes years to complete, they include extension options within their contracts to limit the downside risk of not achieving their desired zoning.

If you want an option to extend the due diligence process, the seller will likely request that either an option fee be paid or that some, if not all, of your earnest money deposit go hard. This means that, if you back out of the contract during the extension period, you will forfeit some or all your deposit to the seller. Because of this, only consider including this provision if you absolutely believe that you will need it.

Closing costs

Along with your down payment amount, you will likely incur additional costs prior to closing on your commercial property. These expenditures are called *"closing costs"* and both the buyer and seller will be responsible for a portion of the final amount. To start, the buyer's closing costs typically include some or all of the following:

- *Loan Origination*
- *Appraisal*

- *Phase I, II and/or III Environmental Report*
- *Structural Engineering Report*
- *Zoning Report*
- *Title Insurance*
- *Legal Fees*
- *As well as many more…*

The sum of these costs is typically between 2-5% of the Purchase Price. On the seller's side, some of the costs may include:

- *Real Estate Commissions*
- *Property Transfer Tax*
- *Recording of the Deed*
- *Legal Fees*
- *Mortgage Payoff*
- *As well as many more…*

The fees paid by each party vary from state to state. Because of this, it's important to ask your commercial real estate agent which fees you will be expected to pay.

Carefully review the document

Once you and your real estate advisory team have drafted a well thought out purchase contract, carefully review the document to ensure you understand the language within the agreement. A purchase contract is a legally binding document so once both parties sign on the dotted line, you must abide by the terms of the agreement. If you come across language that you don't fully understand, reach out to your commercial real estate attorney for clarification. Even if it costs you money to do so, it's worth the price to avoid potential heartache.

Action Items

1) *Work with your real estate advisory team to craft a well thought out offer.*
   a. *Speak with your lender, inspector, and other parties involved in the process to ensure you're requesting enough time for your contingency period.*
2) *Carefully review the final purchase contract to ensure that you fully understand its contents.*
   a. *Once you sign your name on the dotted line, you must adhere to the terms of the agreement.*

CHAPTER 8
NEGOTIATING THE PURCHASE CONTRACT

"Place a higher priority on discovering what a win looks like for the other person." – **Harvey Robbins**

Now that you've drafted and reviewed your final purchase contract, it's time to submit your proposal to the seller. Although there are times where the seller will accept your first offer, it's often not the case. Typically, there will be discussions between both parties until an acceptable agreement is reached. Although this can be a contentious interaction, it doesn't have to be. In this section, we will highlight some of the best strategies you can employ to negotiate a favorable purchase agreement.

Understanding the seller's motivation

This is the most important piece of information you can uncover during the negotiation process. A seller's motivation will indicate how receptive they will be to your offer. A motivated seller is one who has a strong need, not simply a desire, to sell their property. Their need to sell often motivates them to agree to more favorable terms for the buyer. There are many reasons why an owner may be motivated to sell. Some of them may include:

- They're behind on their mortgage payments.
- They're delinquent on their property taxes.
- The property is in poor condition and needs repairs.
- The property was inherited, and the heirs have no desire to keep it.
- They're interested in retiring and the property is the only thing keeping them from doing so.
- As well as many more…

One of the best ways to determine the seller's motivation is to have your commercial real estate agent ask the listing agent. Although they're usually tight lipped, some will openly share this information with you. Next, search the public records to determine how long the seller has owned the property, what they purchased it for, and if any tax delinquencies exist. Your commercial real estate agent should be able to execute these searches on your behalf.

Finally, walk through the property with a commercial contractor to assess the scope of work that will need to be performed. If the property is in a state of disrepair, it may be an indication that the property owner is unable or unwilling to improve the property. In these instances, you can modify your negotiation strategy to focus on the work that will need to be performed to get the property up to an acceptable condition.

By compiling relevant property data, you paint a clearer picture of what the seller may be thinking, and the pain points they are likely dealing with. From there, you can create a compelling offer that addresses the seller's problems while also satisfying your needs of securing the property with favorable terms.

> **Pro-tip:** One of the best books I've read about negotiation is *"Never Split the Difference"* by Christopher Voss. I've used his strategies, particularly negotiating with empathy, deep listening, and using emotion rather than just reason, to effectively negotiate several favorable lease and purchase contracts for my clients. For a copy of the book, check out the link provided here: https://amzn.to/2RY8MDw

Be willing to compromise

Although this is a simple concept, it's one that's often overlooked. I've met many business owners and investors who take the *"my way or the highway"* approach to negotiating. They're so rigid in their desires and are often unwilling to compromise. Because of this, the deal usually falls apart and both parties are left frustrated with the other. Understand that negotiating a contract is a two-way street. Both you and the seller want to have their desires met. Therefore, to work out a deal that satisfies both parties, everyone in the transaction must be willing to compromise.

As an example, if you require more time to seek financing, consider increasing your earnest money deposit to show good faith. If you would like to reduce the final purchase price of the property, don't ask the seller for a significant number of repairs. By giving as well as taking, you convey that you're a serious buyer who wants to reach a mutually acceptable agreement.

Avoid retrading

As you go back and forth, you will eventually settle on an agreement that's acceptable to both parties. Once you reach this point, avoid *"retrading"* on the deal. Retrading is the practice of renegotiating the purchase price of real property by the buyer after initially agreeing to purchase at a higher price. Typically, this occurs during the due diligence period.

Although there are instances where a price reduction may be necessary (i.e., significant structural issues, leaky roof etc.), most of the smaller items (i.e., old furnace, A/C, deferred maintenance items etc.) should be factored into your initial offer. I encourage my clients to do a walkthrough with a licensed general contractor prior to putting the property under contract. That way, you'll have a pretty good idea of what you're getting into prior to investing a significant amount of time, money, and energy into the transaction. The moral of the story is, put in a little bit of effort on the front end to submit a well thought out offer. This approach will help streamline the process of getting to the closing table.

Action Items

1) Work with your real estate advisory team to compile information on the seller and the property.
    a. Compile documents from your local tax assessor's office, utility companies etc.
2) Be willing to compromise with the other party.
    a. Remember, there is an opportunity cost to not getting a deal done as well.
3) Once you reach an acceptable agreement, avoid retrading on the deal.
    a. Although there are instances where a price reduction may be necessary (i.e., significant structural issues, leaky roof etc.), most of the smaller items should be factored into your initial offer.

CHAPTER 9
PERFORMING DUE DILIGENCE

"Buying a property today is a complex process, but that in no way excuses a buyer from their obligation for due diligence." – **Henry Paulson**

Congratulations on getting your commercial property under contract! You're one step closer to commercial real estate ownership. However, now the real work begins. During the rest of your contingency period, you will conduct *"due diligence"* to assess the property's physical condition and, if applicable, its financial performance. In this chapter, we will provide you with a step-by-step process to help you do just that.

Document important dates within the contract

As we mentioned in the previous chapter, commercial contracts can contain various contingency timelines. These periods typically run co-currently and range from 30-90 days or more. Your earnest money deposit will go *"hard"* (i.e., be distributed to the seller) if you back out of the contract after your contingency periods have expired. That's why it's critical that, once the purchase agreement is fully executed, you and your real estate team document the key contingency deadlines.

Typically, the clock starts when all parties have signed the contract. Therefore, if you submit a signed purchase agreement on July 7th and the seller signs and returns it to you on July 9th, the latter date will be day 0 of the timeline.

Once you've determined the starting date, confirm whether the timeline within your contract references *"business days"* or *"calendar days"*. This is a common mistake I've seen many make in the past. If a contract was fully executed on January 1st, 2021, and the contingency deadline is 45 calendar days away, the deadline would fall on February 15th. However, if the contract referenced 45 *"business"* days, your deadline would have fallen on March 9th. That's a 22-day difference!

Although your contingency end dates may seem like a long way away, they creep up on you quickly. For this reason, I highly recommend setting reminders in your calendar for each of your contingency deadlines. Additionally, share these dates with your real estate advisory team and your commercial lender so they too can be held accountable. Employing this strategy will help you avoid overshooting the timeline and forfeiting your earnest money deposit to the seller.

> **Pro-tip:** Your purchase contract may also specify that, if the deadline falls on a holiday or weekend, the true end date will be the following business day. To confirm this, please review your existing agreement with your commercial real estate agent and real estate attorney.

Hiring a commercial property inspector

Probably the easiest and most effective way to perform a physical inspection of a commercial building is to hire a licensed commercial property inspector. A commercial property inspector is a highly trained professional who is skilled at assessing the exterior and interior condition of commercial properties. An experienced commercial inspector will have worked on a variety of property types including office, multifamily, industrial, retail etc. As part of the inspection process, they will examine important components of the building including, but not limited to:

- *Furnaces*
- *A/C Units*
- *Water Heaters*
- *Elevators*
- *Boilers*
- *Roof & Siding*
- *Structure*
- *As well as much more…*

Once their assessment is complete, they will present you with a written report that documents their findings. If additional screening is required, they will recommend that various service professionals (i.e., electricians, HVAC technicians, roofers etc.) perform a more invasive diagnostic.

As you begin your search for a property inspector, make sure they're well versed in assessing the condition of commercial buildings. Unlike residential real estate where most building components are similar, commercial buildings vary widely. Depending on the building's usage, the inspector may have to inspect commercial lifts, bay doors, restaurant components, elevators etc. If they don't know what to look out for, it could spell big trouble for you and your business. Given the complexity of the process, commercial property inspections tend to cost more than residential ones. Having said that, the few extra hundred dollars in cost could save you thousands, if not tens of thousands of dollars in unexpected repair and maintenance expenses.

Inspecting the property on your own

Although I don't usually recommend this approach, there are instances where business owners prefer to be in the driver's seat when it comes to inspecting their commercial property. Depending on the property's size and scope, you may need to solicit the services of an electrician, plumber, roofer, HVAC technician, elevator technician, structural engineer etc. Because of the quantity of service professionals, you'll likely need to work with, I highly encourage you ask your commercial real estate agent for a list of contacts and schedule a time to meet with each individual on-site. Be sure to communicate your intentions to the property owner so they are aware of dates and times these inspections will occur.

After each service professional performs their assessment, speak with them about their findings. Carefully document the most important items and have them send you an email that outlines their professional opinion. You'll want to carefully review this information with your commercial real estate agent prior to the end of your due diligence timeline.

> **Pro-tip:** I've created an excel spreadsheet that highlights some of the major components of a commercial building. To access the file, go to www.raphaelcollazo.com/resources.

Getting clear on your construction budget

As you perform your physical inspections, it's important to get clear on your construction budget. As referenced in the *"Assembling Your Real Estate Advisory Team"*, you should have interviewed several commercial contractors and selected your top 3. During your due diligence period, have each one walk through the space and ask them to provide you with bids for the work.

As you receive each one, scrutinize them rigorously. If you don't understand why a particular line item is included, ask for clarification on its necessity. Sometimes, contractors charge for work that's above and beyond what you want completed. If this is the case, you can choose to either remove the line item, perform the task yourself and/or defer the work to a later date.

Although it may be tempting to choose the discount contractor, I often recommend my clients select the middle quote. This is because a discounted price is often a reflection of their lack of proper experience and/or a track record of success. More often than not, the middle quote is one that properly compensates the general contractor for their experience while not building in the fluff charged by much larger contractors with significant overhead (i.e., employees, a large office lease etc.).

Once you select your contractor, coansider adding 10-15% on top of your quote to account for any delays and/or issues that may arise during the project. Regardless of how great your GC is, it's impossible to predict the future. Therefore, factoring in a buffer amount will help mitigate issues that may arise throughout the renovation.

> **Pro-tip:** Unlike residential construction, commercial construction projects often have a higher price tag. For this reason, understand you will likely experience some sticker shock when you see these commercial quotes for the first time. If you're handy, consider doing some of the work yourself. By performing less complex tasks on your own, you can save yourself hundreds if not thousands of dollars. Examples of these jobs may include doing your own demo work, painting, and priming walls, changing lighting fixtures etc.

Performing Financial Analysis

The next piece of the puzzle is to perform a financial analysis for the property. In most instances, business owners will buy a vacant building to occupy. However, there are instances where a building has tenants, and a business owner occupies a portion of the space. Regardless of which route you take, there are several financial items to consider. In this chapter, we will highlight how to compile the appropriate data so you can make the best decision possible for your business.

Reviewing property data

The first step in the process is to determine your yearly financial obligation for maintaining the property. To accomplish this goal, you'll want to request several pieces of information. These include, but are not limited to:

1) ***Trailing 12 months of water and utility bills*** – *These values may be higher or lower depending on your business use.*

2) ***Service contracts for major mechanicals*** – *Request that the seller provide you with their contracts for recurring service to major mechanicals (i.e., HVAC system, elevators, boilers etc.). This will ensure that service is being performed and what the cost will be each month going forward.*

3) ***Receipts for any recent repairs/maintenance items*** – *Properties need constant maintenance to ensure they last. As a result, you'll want to verify that the owner is up to date on repairs and maintenance items and that they hired reputable professionals to perform the work.*

4) **Age of "big-ticket items" on the premises** – Building components deteriorate over time. Therefore, it's critical to clarify the age of major systems so you can set aside money to replace them in the future. These components include elevators, HVAC Systems, Roofs, Boilers, Water Heaters etc.

5) **Prior 3 years of property taxes** - Check your local tax assessor's office to get an idea of what property tax rates will be once you take possession of the property. In some states, property assessments recalculate when a sale occurs while others recalculate on specific time intervals (i.e. 5, 10, 15 years etc.).

6) **Condo or Association Documents (if applicable)** – If the property is part of a condo or other association, request copies of pertinent condo documents including, but not limited to, bylaws, P&L Statement, Rent Roll etc.

Your commercial real estate agent should be able to help you compile these documents as well as any additional information that may be pertinent to your property assessment. Once you have this information in hand, review the documents with your real estate advisory team. If anything seems out of the ordinary, ask for clarification from the seller. Depending on your findings, you may use this information to request a price adjustment to your purchase contract.

> **Pro-tip:** If the property has been vacant for a while, the landlord may not have up to date receipts for utility charges and other relevant documents. However, you

can still contact your local utility companies to get an average for the area. Additionally, call different service professionals to get a feel for recurring maintenance expenses. Reference the list of contacts provided to you by your commercial real estate agent to compile this data.

Reviewing Tenant Data (if applicable)

If the property has tenants, there are additional steps you'll need to take. To start, get clear on the relationship between the current landlord and tenants. To accomplish your goal, you will need to request *"estoppel agreements"* for each tenant. Estoppel agreements (also known as estoppel certificates) are legal documents used to verify certain representations made by the landlord. These are typically requested during the due diligence process and contain verbiage referencing how much the tenant pays in rent, if there are any security deposits (and where they are held), the expiration date of the agreement, etc. Essentially, it highlights the terms of the agreement between the landlord and the tenant.

Additionally, it should clarify that neither the landlord nor the lessee owes money to the other. For example, if the landlord is responsible for replacing major mechanical components within the building and due to the landlord's inaction, the tenant is forced to replace their own water heater, the landlord may owe the tenant over $1,000. If a signed estoppel agreement is not presented to the tenant during the due diligence period, the tenant may decide to sue the new owner for the balance once they take possession of the property.

Typically, your purchase contract should request that all signed estoppel agreements be provided to you within 2-4 weeks of the contract execution date. Having said that, you should ensure that you receive these signed documents well in advance of the expiration date of your due diligence period. That way, you have time to address any discrepancies that arise and, if necessary, back out of the contract without forfeiting your earnest money deposit. Work with your commercial real estate agent to ensure these documents are collected in a timely manner.

Finally, request that the landlord provide you with any pertinent financial documents they have for the property. These documents may include, but are not limited to:

- *Trailing 12 Months (TTM)*
- *Profit & Loss Statement (P&L)*
- *Capital Expenditures Report*
- *Repair & Maintenance Report*
- *As well as much more...*

Review each one to get an understanding of the financial performance of the property and what capital outlays will need to be planned for in the future. During your analysis, pay particular attention to the collection and expense data. If anything seems out of the ordinary, ask for clarification from the seller. Like the physical inspection of the property, you may use this information to request a price adjustment to your purchase contract or, if the discrepancies are stark enough, decide that it's best to walk away from the opportunity.

Environmental assessments

Another critical part of the due diligence process is assessing the property's environmental condition. Environmental issues are scary to potential buyers as they are often extremely expensive to remedy. Because of this, you must solicit the services of an environmental engineering company to perform an environmental assessment. There are several environmental assessments that can be performed. Below, I've provided an overview of each:

Phase I

A phase 1 assessment is the least invasive of all the assessments. The inspection process typically includes:

- *A site visit to see what's in the neighborhood.*
- *A historical review of site to determine its current and prior uses.*
- *A full regulatory review which includes the examination of local, state, and federal files as well as neighboring sites to determine potential contamination.*

Most commercial lenders will require that a Phase I assessment be performed. Additionally, your lender may not accept an environmental report secured in advance by the seller. To identify reputable environmental engineering firms, ask your commercial real estate agent and commercial lender as they will likely have several to recommend. If a Phase I assessment is performed and your property passes inspection, the engineering firm will submit a report to your lender signing off on the site. However, if the potential of contaminants exists or if any are identified, a more invasive environmental analysis (Phase II) may be required.

Phase II

A Phase II assessment is a more invasive inspection that typically includes:

- *Sampling of the soil and performing a laboratory analysis.*
- *Checking the groundwater on-site and around the premises.*
- *Performing an assessment of potential problems and their long-term effects.*
- *Providing possible remediation actions.*

As part of a Phase II assessment, soil samples are extracted from different spots on the property and at different depths. These samples are then sent to a laboratory for testing to determine what dangerous chemicals, if any, are present in the ground. Depending on the level of contamination that exists, their report will recommend a course of action to deal with the problem. Because a Phase II assessment can be relatively expensive, its cost often becomes a negotiable item between the seller and the buyer.

Phase III

A Phase III assessment is one where proposed solutions are implemented after site contamination is identified. Some of the actions taken may include:

- *Performing contamination clean up.*
- *Maintaining the status quo as to not alter existing conditions.*
- *Ongoing monitoring of the site to ensure the contamination does not spread.*

Depending on the future use of the site, proposed solutions may vary. For example, a property that will be used as a school may be treated differently than land where a parking lot will be developed. Additionally, there are extreme cases where environmental remediation may cost more than the property is worth. In these instances, walking away from the contract may be the best decision.

Performing a survey

This is probably the most often overlooked part of the due diligence process. A survey is a report issued by a licensed surveyor that confirms land boundaries and identifies other types of restrictions and conditions that apply to the legal description of a property.

Although this report provides valuable information, several of my past clients have pushed back on this item.

During our discussion, they typically say something like, *"Why would I pay $800 or more for someone to tell me where my boundary lines are? I can clearly see the fence, so I don't want to bother with the expense."* Most of the time, surveys confirm what you already know to be true about the property. In these instances, it can feel like commissioning the report was a waste of time and money.

However, survey issues arise more often than you think, and some can be catastrophic to your business. A few years ago, an investor friend of mine shared a story about one of their friends who purchased an industrial property at auction. This property had a large open field in the back that the new owner planned to pave and then market the space for lease. However, after closing on the property, he discovered that the rear parcel was owned by someone else, and his parcel only encompassed the structure and the small front parking lot. Because of this blunder, he's now limited in what potential users he can market to.

Another recent example further illustrates the value of commissioning a survey. An agent in our office represented a client in the acquisition of 20+ acres of land in Louisville, KY. During the due diligence process, the buyer commissioned a survey to define exactly where the property lines fell. Upon receiving the final report, he discovered that the parcel he was under contract to purchase was 30% smaller than had been advertised! As a result, he was able to go back to the seller and get a price adjustment to reflect the reduced acreage.

Although you may be frustrated by the added expense, having clarity of what you're purchasing is worth its weight in gold. Not only that, but if you decide to sell your property in the future, it will be a valuable piece of data to share with prospective buyers.

Reviewing your findings

Once you've performed a complete physical, financial, and environmental analysis of the property, carefully review your findings with your commercial real estate agent. As you comb through the data, some of the questions to ponder include:

1) How much will repairs to the property cost?
2) What large capital expenditures are expected soon (i.e., 1-5 years)?
3) What will the construction cost be to get the space functional for my use?
4) If tenants are present, are they delinquent and do they take care of their space?
5) What lease expiration dates are upcoming?
6) What responsibilities, both legal and financial, do I have to the tenants?
7) As well as others…

If you deem that an adjustment to the contract is warranted, work with your commercial real estate agent to draft an addendum that reflects your desires. This addendum may include references to a price adjustment, repairs to be performed, request for an extension, additional screening costs to be paid by the seller etc. Once you've drafted this document, have your commercial agent submit it to the seller's representative.

Once the seller receives your proposal, they will respond in one of three ways. They can choose to sign the addendum without any modifications, they can counter, or they can outright reject your addendum and not provide any additional feedback.

Regardless of their response, contemplate how you will approach each scenario. If after your analysis, you determine that it's not wise to proceed with the purchase, it's OK to walk away. Although it may seem like you've wasted time and resources without anything to show for it, it's better to cut your losses than purchase a bad deal. Don't be afraid to throw in the towel if moving forward doesn't make sense.

> **Pro-tip:** I cannot stress this enough: don't feel obligated to close on the property if the evidence you uncover does not support doing so. If anyone on your real estate advisory team is pressuring you, reevaluate your relationship with them. Your commercial agent, real estate attorney and accountant have a fiduciary responsibility to you and should always act in your best interest. Remember that your team is serving you and not the other way around.

Action Items

1) Hire a commercial inspector to perform a comprehensive physical inspection of the property.
    a. If you prefer to control the process, hire the appropriate service professionals to provide a comprehensive assessment of the building's physical condition.
2) Request bids from each of your top 3 commercial contractors.
3) Work with your commercial real estate agent to compile all the relevant financial and tenant data for the property.
    a. If anything seems out of the ordinary, seek clarification from the listing agent.
4) Commission an environmental assessment for the property.
    a. If more invasive procedures are required, a price reduction or additional action may be required.
5) Perform a survey to clarify the boundaries of the property.
6) Review your findings and determine what the next course of action will be.
    a. If after reviewing the data, you determine that the property is no longer worth pursuing, don't be afraid to back out of the contract.

CHAPTER 10
WORKING WITH YOUR LENDER

"If everyone is moving forward together then success takes care of itself" – **Henry Ford**

As you perform your due diligence on the property, you will need to work with your lender to secure financing. Although each bank will have their own lending criteria, their core internal processes will likely be similar. Therefore, it's important to understand how banks fund loans so you can present yourself in the best light. In this section, we will highlight some of the documents, processes, and actions you must take to secure the best terms for your commercial loan.

Furnishing financial and property documents

As referenced in the *"Identifying Commercial Lenders"* chapter of the book, you should already be in contact with loan officers at several commercial banks. Now that you have the property under contract, you will need to provide each with a host of financial and property documents. These include, but are not limited to:

1) *Fully Executed Purchase contract for the property*
2) *Personal & Business Financial Statements*
3) *Business Balance Sheet*
4) *3 years of Business and Personal Tax Returns*
5) *If tenants are present, any leases and financial projections*
6) *Construction Budget (if applicable)*
7) *As well as others…*

Once your loan officer has these documents in hand, they will draft a loan application and submit it to their "*underwriting division*". Underwriters are individuals within a lending institution who assess the risk of a loan. They evaluate the financial strength of a borrower and determine how likely they are to repay the debt. If a borrower is strong enough to support the monthly mortgage payments, the loan will be approved, and the funds will be disbursed. Having said that, the final loan amount will depend on several factors. In the next section, we will explain how this process works.

Determining your final mortgage amount

This is probably one of the most common misconceptions regarding commercial lending. While financing residential properties is often straightforward, the process of determining how much to lend on commercial properties can be quite complex. Lenders often use a variety calculations to determine the final mortgage amount. Below I've shared an overview of each:

Loan-to-Value Ratio (LTV)

The first method lenders use to calculate a borrower's final loan amount is the *"Loan-To-Value Ratio"*. The loan-to- value (LTV) ratio compares the total loan amount to the property's appraised value. To better illustrate this point, I've provided the calculation below:

$$LTV = \frac{(Total\ Loan\ Amount)}{(Property's\ Appraised\ Value)}$$

Therefore, if a bank specifies a maximum LTV of 80% on a $1,000,000 property, the maximum loan amount they would issue is $ 800,000. This is by far the most straightforward approach and it may be used in conjunction with the other methods to determine the final loan amount.

Loan to Cost (LTC)

The second method lenders employ is the *"Loan-to-Cost Ratio."* Although similar to a property's *"Loan to Value Ratio,"* it has one major difference. LTC considers the entire project cost, which includes the property's acquisition price as well as the cost of renovation, documentation etc. To illustrate this point, I've provided, the equation below:

$$LTC = \frac{(Total\ Loan\ Amount)}{(Total\ Project\ Cost)}$$

Working with Your Lender

For example, let's imagine that you decide to purchase a commercial building for $1,000,000. After having your contractor walk through the property, you determine you will need to spend $200,000 to renovate the space for your use. When approaching banks, they advertise a maximum LTC of 65%. In this scenario, your maximum loan amount would be:

$$0.65 = \frac{\text{(Total Loan Amount)}}{(\$1,000,000 + \$200,000)}$$

$$\text{Total Loan Amount} = \$780,000$$

This method can be most beneficial to borrowers who have a significant renovation/construction component tied to their acquisition.

Debt Service Coverage Ratio (DSCR)

The third method considered by lenders is your business's *"Debt Service Coverage Ratio"* (DSCR). The DSCR measures the number of times your business's net operating income can cover the annual debt service for the loan. To better illustrate this, I've provided the equation below:

$$\text{D.S.C.R} = \frac{\text{(Net Operating Income)}}{\text{(Yearly Debt Service)}}$$

For example, if a lender requires a 1.3X debt service coverage ratio and your business's projected net operating income in the first year of ownership is $130,000, your annual loan payments cannot exceed the following:

$$1.3 = \frac{\$130,000}{\text{Yearly Debt Service}}$$

$$\text{Yearly Debt Service} = \$100,000$$

The reason lenders have a DSCR requirement is because it gives the borrower a buffer in case their business's income falters. In the case of a 1.3X debt service coverage ratio requirement, a borrower's net operating income would have to drop by a full $30,000 per year before they start having issues paying their mortgage.

Now that you've calculated your yearly debt service, you'll need to determine what the maximum loan amount is. To do this, you can utilize the following equation:

$$\text{Loan Amount} = \frac{PMT}{i} \left[1 - \frac{1}{(1+(i))^n}\right]$$

- PMT is the monthly payment
- i is the interest rate per month in decimal form (interest rate percentage divided by 12)
- n is the number of months (term of the loan in months)

If your lender was offering a loan at a 6% interest rate with a 20-year amortization, the maximum loan amount would be:

$$\text{Loan Amount} = \frac{\$8{,}333.33}{0.06/12} \left[1 - \frac{1}{(1+(0.06/12))^{240}}\right]$$

$$\text{Loan Amount} = \$1{,}163{,}173.10$$

It's important to note that depending on the terms of your loan (i.e., interest rate, amortization etc.), your maximum loan amount will vary. Therefore, use the preliminary loan terms provided to you by each lender to determine what this value could be.

Carefully review your term sheets

Now that your lender has performed an initial review of the documents you provided them, they will send you a *"Term Sheet"* that lays out the characteristics of their loan offering. Although term sheets vary from bank to bank, the most common financial items referenced include:

- **Loan Amount** – *How much the lender is willing to loan you.*
- **Interest Rate** – *How much the borrower will pay each year in interest based on the outstanding loan amount.*
- **Term** – *How long the interest rate will remain fixed. After the term, the interest rate will either float or the note will come due.*

- *Amortization Period* – How long the loan payments will be spread over.

- *Balloon Payment* – A larger-than-usual one-time payment at the end of the loan term. Not all loans have balloon payments.

- *Pre-payment penalties* - A fee that lenders charge borrowers who pay off all or part of their loans ahead of schedule. This provision is used to deter borrowers from refinancing within a certain timeframe.

- *Recourse vs. Non-Recourse* – This provision states whether a lender can go after the borrower's other assets that were not used as collateral for the loan. This may include business & personal assets. If this is your first time securing commercial financing, the loan will likely be recourse.

After receiving term sheets from each lender, work with your commercial real estate agent to compare each offering. Some of the questions to ponder include:

- What will my monthly mortgage payment be?
- What fees are involved with securing the loan?
- Are there any restrictive covenants?
- What are my 1,3,5 and 10-year goals and how does each offering align with them?
- As well as many more…

Once you identify the best one, it may be tempting to accept the terms as is. After all, in residential real estate, what you see is what you get. However, in commercial real estate, everything is negotiable.

Therefore, consider approaching each lender and requesting modifications. This request may include references to a lower interest rate, eliminating pre-payment penalties, extending the term and/or amortization period, lowering the down payment requirement etc. If you're a strong borrower, lenders may compete with one another to win your business.

> **Pro-tip:** Just because a bank quotes you a lower interest rate, the *"Annual Percentage Rate"* (A.P.R) may be higher than other options. The A.P.R of a loan package includes not only the interest expense on the loan but also all the fees and other costs involved in procuring the loan. These fees can include broker fees, closing costs, rebates, discount points etc. Therefore, when speaking with banks, make sure to request an A.P.R value instead of an interest rate.

Communicating with your lender

Once you've negotiated a favorable term sheet and selected your top choice, inform your lender of important dates within your contract. These dates include your financing and closing deadline. Since commercial lenders work on many transactions, having deadlines in place will help them properly manage their workload to achieve a timely closing.

Additionally, if your lender has questions regarding items that are pertinent to the transaction, be sure to respond as quickly as possible. Failure to do so in a timely manner may result in you eclipsing your financing deadline and forfeiting your earnest money deposit to the seller.

Finally, periodically check-in with your lender to confirm that certain back-end processes are being completed. Typically, lenders are responsible for ordering environmental assessments and appraisals. This process can take several days to complete as jobs are put out for bid to an approved list of vendors. If these reports are not ordered in a timely manner, financing can be delayed which can put the transaction in jeopardy. Therefore, work with your lender to define when each report will be ordered. After receiving a response, follow up with them to ensure nothing slips through the cracks.

Action Items

1) Provide each of the lenders on your list with the requested financial and property documents.
   a. Work with your real estate advisory team to ensure the information is accurate.
2) Understand how underwriters calculate the final loan amount for commercial property acquisitions.
3) Carefully review each bank's term sheet and identify the best one.
   a. Consider negotiating with several banks to achieve the best loan terms.
4) Periodically check-in with your lender to ensure important milestones are met.
   a. If your lender has questions regarding items pertinent to the transaction, respond in a timely manner.

CHAPTER 11
ADDRESSING PRE-CLOSING ITEMS

"Resistance is the greatest just before the finish line." – **Steven Pressfield**

You're rounding the corner and entering the home stretch! All your hard work is about to pay off. However, before heading to the closing table, there are several actions left to take. In this section, we will highlight some of the most important pre-closing items and share step-by-step processes you can use to accomplish each one.

Attaining proper licensing & permits

Regardless of what business you're in, you will likely be required to secure permits and/or licenses to operate. The most common and widely used is a *"business license"*. In the U.S., all businesses must secure a business license to operate legally. The reason for this is that states must be able to identify your business so they can keep track of your finances for tax purposes as well as ensure you're held accountable for your actions.

To find out where to get your business license, google your city's name followed by the words *"business license"* and/

or check the US Small Business Administration (SBA) website for details. Often you can simply follow the application procedures laid out on your state government's website or go to city hall and pick them up in person. You'll need to renew this license periodically, so track the deadlines by setting a reminder in your calendar.

Other required licenses and permits will depend on what industry you're in. For example, if you plan on opening a restaurant, you'll need food service licenses, food handler's permits and potentially a liquor license if you plan on serving liquor on site. If you operate a logistics company that utilizes semi-trucks, you'll likely need transportation/logistics permits to operate oversized and overweight vehicles. Because of this variability, it's important to do your own independent research to determine what permits and licenses are required for your industry. For a link to a helpful article on this topic, I've provided a link below:

Licenses & Permits: https://bit.ly/2ETUBZC

Creating signage for your business

Although this section applies to all industries, it's especially important if you have a retail component to your business. The benefit of having signage on site is that it alerts potential customers that you're open for business. If you're located along a high traffic roadway, having a well-placed and attention-grabbing sign can translate into significant foot-traffic for your business. Although it would be nice to hang a sign wherever you please, cities usually have regulations that dictate where signs can be placed on the premises, their height and width as well as how high they can be off the ground.

To find out this information, call city hall and/or visit their website. Since they're the ones responsible for issuing signage permits, they will provide you with up-to-date information on what rules apply to your unique situation. Having said that, I generally recommend my clients cut out the middleman and call various sign companies around town. Since sign companies create and hang signs for a living, they often know exactly what is and isn't allowed in any given area around town. Not only that, but you're able to compile multiple bids and see which company offers you the best price and quality of service.

Securing commercial insurance

Before finalizing your purchase, your lender will require you to have building insurance in place. When it comes to insurance, it pays to shop around. However, identifying multiple insurance carriers and getting quotes from each can be extremely time consuming. For that reason, I often recommend my clients solicit the services of a competent and qualified *"commercial insurance broker"*. Commercial insurance brokers are individuals who work with you to determine your insurance needs and shop a host of different carriers to get you the appropriate coverage for the best possible rate. There are a few benefits to using one.

First, they save you a significant amount of time. An experienced commercial insurance broker will have a long list of insurance carriers they've worked with in the past. Because of their familiarity with each carrier's offerings, they can streamline the review process and help you select the best coverage much faster than you could on your own.

Second, because they have pre-existing relationships with these carriers, you may get a much better price than shopping direct. Insurance companies often provide brokers with lower rates because they are professionally trained to accurately assess risk. As a result, a broker's clients usually present a lower risk to the carrier than those who secure insurance independently.

Third, they will be your point of contact for all your insurance related questions. Unlike large insurance companies that are known for being impersonal and difficult to get ahold of, your insurance broker will be available to answer your questions any time of day. I've had clients who have contacted their broker on nights and weekends. They received a prompt response, and the issues were resolved soon thereafter. If your commercial insurance broker is committed, they'll be there for you when you need them most.

Finally, they are 100% free for you to use! Like your commercial real estate agent, your commercial insurance broker is paid a commission by the carrier they ultimately pair you with. This means that you get the benefit of working with an expert in the insurance industry, without having to pay for their services. It's really a no brainer.

To find a great commercial insurance broker, start by asking your commercial real estate agent if they have any recommendations. Since they deal in the commercial arena every day, they will likely have a few they can refer to you. Along with that, ask your friends who are small business owners. If they're happy with their insurance broker, they will happily refer them to you. Once you have a list of potential candidates, call each one and ask them to provide you with a list of carriers they work with. Compare the lists, identify 2 agents who have differing carriers, and ask them to compile quotes for you. From there, choose the one who offers you the appropriate coverage for the best rate.

Carefully review your closing statement

Several days prior to closing, you will receive a closing statement from your lender that outlines all debits and credits for both the buyer and seller. When you receive this document, carefully review it with your commercial real estate agent. Verify all prorations (i.e., taxes, condo fees, rents (if any) etc.) are calculated correctly. Additionally, make sure that the fees to be paid by both parties are specified correctly.

Finally, if your lender agreed to reduce or eliminate certain fees to win your business, make sure it's reflected in the closing statement. A few years ago, my client decided to work with a bank who promised to pay ½ the appraisal fee for a retail investment property he was purchasing. When the closing statement arrived, it stated that he was responsible for paying the full amount. Luckily, we caught this mistake and informed the lender. By taking 10 minutes to review the document, my client saved several thousands of dollars. Once you've confirmed that everything on the closing statement is correct, send an email confirmation to the parties involved.

Getting to the closing table

The last step in the process is to perform a final walkthrough. You should plan to do this 1-2 days before closing. Your objective is to ensure that the property's physical condition is the same or better than when you performed your inspection. Additionally, if any repairs were requested, this is your chance to verify that the work was performed to an acceptable standard. As you walk through the property, make note of anything that looks out of the ordinary.

Once complete, discuss any irregularities with your commercial real estate agent. If necessary, send a detailed email to the listing agent explaining your concerns. Include pictures, repair documents and any other relevant information to provide context. You will want to resolve these items prior to closing on the property. If this can't be achieved, a credit may be warranted.

On the day of closing, speak with your commercial real estate agent about what you need to bring. Some of these items may include, a government issued photo ID (i.e., driver's license, passport etc.), cashier's check for all necessary payments etc. As part of the process, you'll be asked to sign various documents including, but not limited to, assignments and assumption of leases, deeds, environmental reports and assignments of liability, zoning disclosures and warranties, and anything else the law requires and/or the parties decide is necessary to close the deal.

Additionally, your lender will require you to sign a host of financial documents pertaining to the sale. These may include, a promissory note, mortgage, transfer tax declaration etc. If you have any questions regarding the verbiage contained in any of these documents, don't hesitate to ask your commercial lender. You should never sign something you don't understand as it could come back to bite you in the future.

Once you've reviewed and signed the required documents, the seller or seller's agent will provide you with the keys to your new commercial property! Although this may be the end of the road for some of you, others will need to address the interior and/or exterior renovation of the building. In the next section, we will explore how to do just that.

> **Pro-tip:** Verify that the names of all property owners are spelled correctly and that any other inaccuracies are addressed. If any discrepancies are identified, communicate this to the closing attorney or escrow agent. From there, they will typically request that you sign a document allowing them to correct these issues after closing. They will then provide you with a copy and changes will be made within a specified period.

Action Items

1) *Register for a business license and do research on what other licenses and/or permits your business needs to legally operate.*
    a. *Maintaining these licenses and/or permits will likely be a recurring expense. Because of this, make sure you have funds set aside in your budget to cover these expenses.*
2) *Call at least 3 different sign companies and request bids from each.*
    a. *Along with that, ask them to confirm what the sign restrictions are for your property.*
3) *Ask your commercial real estate agent and other business owners who they recommend as a commercial insurance broker.*
    a. *Call each one and ask them to provide you with a list of carriers they affiliate with.*
    b. *Compare the lists and select 2 brokers who have differing carriers.*
    c. *Have each provide you with bids and choose the one that offers you the appropriate coverage for the best rate.*
4) *Carefully review the closing statement and ensure all debits and credits are allocated correctly.*
    a. *If your lender agreed to reduce or eliminate certain fees to win your business, make sure it's reflected in the closing statement.*

5) Perform a final walkthrough before closing on the property.
    a. Document any irregularities and send a detailed overview of your findings to the listing agent.
    b. Fight to resolve these outstanding items before closing but, if this can't be achieved, request a credit.
6) Carefully review all documents that are provided to you at closing.
    a. If you don't understand something, seek clarification.

CHAPTER 12
COMPLETING YOUR BUILD-OUT

"Quality is never an accident. It is always the result of intelligent effort." – **John Ruskin**

In the *"Performing Due Diligence"* chapter of the book, you selected a commercial contractor after reviewing the bids provided to you by your top 3 choices. Now that you've made your decision, it's time to sit down with them to review several items. In this section, we'll explain how to work with your general contractor to ensure the project remains on time and on budget.

Sticking to your timeline and budget

The first step in the process is to clearly define project milestones and expectations. If your contractor is experienced, they will likely create a visual representation of this timeline, known as a *"Gantt chart"*, to provide more clarity. A Gantt chart is one that depicts the project work to be completed over various stages of the project life cycle. To better illustrate this document, I've provided an example below:

As you can see, the type of activity, start date, duration and end date of each step are provided. This ensures that everyone is on the same page and that the expectations are clearly defined. Once the project begins, continually check-in to make sure you're on track to hit the target completion date. Periodically swing by the site at different times of the day to see how the work is progressing. If you see something out of the ordinary, bring it to the attention of your GC. Although most great contractors will have a handle on this, you need to take an active role on the project to ensure it stays on track.

If issues do arise, work with your GC to remedy the situation. This may include updating the Gantt chart to reflect delays and/or coordinating with new sub-contractors to perform the work. Finally, if your GC continually fails to address your concerns and prove themselves incapable of getting the job done, it may be wise to terminate the contract and move on to another candidate. Although this may be a difficult conversation to have, it's better to cut your losses and move on. Remember, if you properly vet your commercial GC on the front-end, you will likely avoid having to deal with this scenario.

> **Pro-tip:** I recommend structuring your agreement with your contractor whereby the disbursements are issued whenever a milestone is hit on the project timeline. This helps limit the risk of a contractor receiving most of the money upfront and not completing the work. For example, if you begin a $100,000 renovation for a retail store, you may provide $20,000 to your contractor upfront to purchase materials and hire the initial subcontractors. Once they reach the next milestone and you're satisfied with the quality of their work, you would make the next disbursement. This would continue until the project is complete and the final disbursement is issued.

Action Items

1) *Clearly define project timelines for each component of the construction process.*
   a. *Have your commercial contractor provide you with a Gantt or some other form of visual representation of the timeline.*
2) *Periodically show up on site to ensure the work is being completed properly.*
3) *If your GC continues to miss deadlines, consider seeking the services of another commercial contractor.*
   a. *Although the discussion may be uncomfortable, you will save yourself a ton of future heartache.*

CHAPTER 13
OPENING YOUR DOORS!

"Always deliver more than expected."
– **Larry Page**

Congratulations on finalizing the purchase and renovation of your new commercial property! It's a huge accomplishment and you should be proud of your progress thus far. Although this may feel like the end of the road, the real work is about to begin. For the rest of your time in business, you must effectively manage your operation to support your family, develop your team members and make a positive impact in your community. Although this is not a comprehensive list, below I've provided some of the most common real estate related items to consider throughout your ownership.

Creating a list of important dates and contacts

Once you complete the transaction, it's important to keep a *"cheat sheet"* of important dates and information that is pertinent to complying with your future obligations. Below I've provided a few of the most common:

- *Mortgage payment date*
- *Mortgage amount*
- *Property Tax Due Date*
- *General maintenance contract dates*
- *Loan term end date*
- *As well as much more…*

Work with your real estate advisory team to ensure it's comprehensive. Once you complete your list, hang it up somewhere you can reference it regularly. Additionally, consider programming these dates into your calendar so you're notified whenever one is upcoming.

Finally, ask your real estate advisory team to provide you with a list of qualified commercial contacts who can help you with the future maintenance needs of your property. These professionals may include HVAC technicians, Plumbers, Roofers, handymen etc. I regularly provide my clients with a list of vetted professionals who I've worked with in the past. Your commercial agent will likely have a similar list to share with you.

Accounting for future capital expenses

Over time, your commercial property will experience normal wear and tear. As a result, it's important to set aside funds each month to account for regular property maintenance. Some of these services may include:

- **A/C and Furnace** – Bi-annually
- **Elevator** – Monthly/Bi-annually
- **Landscaping** – Weekly/Monthly
- **Painting** – Every few years
- **As well as much more...**

Additionally, you'll want to set aside funds to account for large capital expenditures. Some of these items may involve repairing and/or replacing:

- Roof & Gutters
- HVAC system
- Elevators
- Water Heaters/Boilers
- Bay & Dock Doors
- Industrial Refrigerators & Freezers
- As well as much more...

To start, create a separate bank account at your preferred bank and set up a recurring monthly transfer. For most properties, allocating between 1-5% of property value each year should cover most expenses.

Finally, I recommend creating a checklist of these items and hanging it somewhere you can reference it regularly. Additionally, consider programming these dates into your calendar so you're notified whenever one is upcoming. This will ensure these items stay top of mind and that you address them in a timely manner. Remember, the better you take care of your property, the longer it will last and the better resale value it will have.

Planning your future

As a passionate and driven entrepreneur, your future business goals likely include expanding your operations and positively impacting as many lives as possible. Because of this, it's important to create and regularly review your 1,3,5 and 10-year goals to determine how your real estate needs will evolve. Read local and national business journals to keep abreast of new real estate trends. Perform market studies to determine which areas of the country are most promising for future expansion. Along with that, periodically check-in with your commercial real estate agent. Not only will they provide you with an update on the real estate market, they will also happily refer you to anyone in their network who can help your business grow and succeed.

Keep in touch

Now that you've made it to the end of this book, be sure to keep us in mind for your future real estate needs! If you're located in Louisville, KY and its surrounding areas, I'd be honored to help you identify, analyze, negotiate and purchase your next commercial property. You can contact me via email at raphael@fidelitydevelopmentcompany.com and/or my cell at (502) 536-7315.

Even if you're not located in Louisville, I encourage you to reach out anyway! I'd be happy to share whatever insights I have as well as connect you with high-performing professionals in your area who can help you secure a commercial space that's right for you. I wish you and your business continued success in the future!

> **Note from the author:** If you enjoyed this book, I would greatly appreciate if you could leave a 5-star review on Amazon. Reviews are gold to authors, and they ensure that more business owners like you can benefit from the information provided. Below, I've provided the link to leave a review:
> *Give a 5-star Review for Before Buy That Building.*

BIO

R aphael Collazo is a licensed commercial real estate agent specializing in retail and industrial properties. Transitioning from a career in software, Raphael brings a strong technical background and a love for dissecting complex problems to his client interactions. These characteristics enable him to provide innovative and effective real estate solutions to help his clients get the most out of each transaction. As a real estate investor himself, Raphael is acutely aware of what investors look for when evaluating commercial property. As a result, he's able to offer a unique perspective and help his clients make the best possible decision based on their business and financial goals.

Prior to joining the Grisanti Group, Raphael worked as a software implementation consultant for FAST Enterprises, a software company that provides C.O.T.S software products to government agencies. Having lived and worked in various locations around the United States and abroad including Pordenone, Italy, Phoenix, Arizona, Washington D.C, San Juan, Puerto Rico and Louisville Kentucky, Raphael has gained a unique understanding of cultural intricacies and has leveraged those experiences to expand his professional network to better serve his clients.

Along with being a full-time commercial real estate agent, Raphael is also the author of the Millennial Playbook series, a book series which focuses on personal and professional development topics for young professionals. As a performance coach and speaker, he's also had the opportunity to speak to thousands of students and professionals on a wide range of subjects. Raphael graduated from Arizona State University in 2013 with a bachelor's degree in industrial engineering and a minor in economics.

BOOK RECOMMENDATIONS

Although this book is a comprehensive guide to purchasing commercial real estate, it's most certainly not the only one that offers valuable insights to business owners. For that reason, I've dedicated this section to highlighting other outstanding books that will help you along your entrepreneurial journey. If you would like to recommend any business/entrepreneurship books that you found valuable, feel free to reach out! I'm always looking for great reads to expand my knowledge.

The Due-Diligence Handbook for Commercial Real Estate – Brian Hennessey

With over 35 years of experience in the commercial real estate space, Brian has managed every aspect of the real estate transaction: from developing acquisition and disposition strategies to conducting market and feasibility analyses; negotiating and executing leases and multi-state portfolio transactions totaling approximately 12 million square feet at values in excess of $2 billion. Given his vast experience, he has a wealth of knowledge to draw upon.

Since writing this book back in 2012, he has made a name for himself teaching others how to properly perform due diligence on commercial property. As a business owner, it's your job to inspect the mechanicals, structure, roof and other building components prior to taking possession of your space. With this book as your guide, you can help mitigate the risk of major building components failing throughout your ownership. If you're interested in purchasing the book, I've provided the link here: https://amzn.to/3a2S6jd

The Miracle Morning – Hal Elrod

This is one of the most profound books I've ever read. Although it's not a traditional business book, its one that I recommend to all my clients and friends. Hal's life has been filled with ups and downs. At the age of 20, he was struck head on by a drunk driver and flatlined for 6 minutes. His doctors thought he would never walk again but Hal was committed to proving them wrong. After achieving a miraculous recovery, he went on to become one of the top salesmen at his company and the future looked bright. However, after the 2008 financial crisis, he lost it all and once again found himself in a deep depression.

What got him out of his funk, was establishing a morning routine. His routine consisted of 6 key components which include meditation, affirmation, visualization, exercise, reading and journaling. Since incorporating this routine into my morning, my life has drastically changed for the better. I credit this practice for enabling me to write 6 books on a variety of topics. Additionally, by reading each morning, I've been able to complete over 200 books within a 5-year period. If I continue following this practice, who knows what the future holds! If you're interested in purchasing the book, I've provided the link here: https://amzn.to/30YedHt

The Ride of a Lifetime – Bob Iger

This is another classic biography that has so many great lessons on leadership and growing an iconic brand. Bob Iger, former CEO and Chairman of the Walt Disney corporation, documents his rise from humble beginnings to the pinnacle of one of the most recognizable companies in the world. He provides insights on the challenges he faced and the decision-making process he employed to expand Disney's footprint in the world of entertainment.

I loved this book because it's so applicable to entrepreneurs, regardless of your industry. We all face challenges in our business, and many require us to evolve as a person to address them. Bob shares the many revelations he experienced throughout his career, so we don't have to do the heavy lifting over again. If you're interested in purchasing the book, I've provided the link here: https://amzn.to/2ZsGQf5

Never Split the Difference – Chris Voss

Have you ever wondered how some people seem to get their way regardless of the circumstances? It's like no matter how dire the situation, they always come out on top. Well after reading *"Never Split the Difference"* by Chris Voss, I can see how someone can develop the skills necessary to become an excellent negotiator.

Chris Voss, a former FBI hostage negotiator, regularly found himself in untenable situations. As part of his job, he had to negotiate with terrorists and highly dangerous individuals to secure the release of hostages. There was no compromising in these scenarios as doing so meant either injury or death. To accomplish his goal, Chris used a variety of negotiation techniques including active listening, tactical empathy, mirroring, labeling etc. to bring the other party over to his way of thinking.

I found this book extremely insightful as its applicable to anyone. Regardless of your background, you will face a situation where you must negotiate with another party. Examples may include salary negotiations with your employer, contract negotiations with a prospective client, negotiations when purchasing a car, convincing your child to eat their vegetables etc. By utilizing these techniques, you will improve your batting average as a negotiator which, over time, will lead to an improvement in a variety of areas of your life. After reading this book, I've used Chris's techniques to negotiate several favorable lease and purchase contracts for my clients. If you're interested in purchasing the book, I've provided the link here: https://amzn.to/2RY8MDw

REAL ESTATE TERMINOLOGY

To properly digest the content of this book, it's important to understand the terminology that is regularly used in the commercial real estate industry. For that reason, I decided to dedicate this section to highlighting some of the most common commercial real estate terms, phrases, and expressions. By learning these, you'll have the proper framework to assess the merits of a commercial property and maximize the value you receive from the transaction.

> **Disclaimer:** Depending on the context, some of these terms may have more than one definition. Because this book discusses purchasing commercial real estate, this is the lens I used when describing the terms.

Add on Factor: The percentage of a building's gross usable space that is added to each tenant's rented space to determine their total rent.

Adjusted Basis: The original cost or other basis of a property, minus the depreciation deductions and increased by capital expenditures. For example, let's imagine that someone buys a lot for $100,000. They then build a retail facility on it for $600,000. Finally, they depreciate the improvements for tax purposes at the rate of $15,000 per year. After three years, the adjusted basis of the property would be $655,000 [$100,000 + $600,000 - (3 x $15,000)].

Amortization: The paying off of debt over time in equal installments.

Annual Percentage Rate (A.P.R) – A value expressed as a percentage that represents the actual yearly cost of funds over the term of a loan. This includes any fees or additional costs associated with the transaction, but it does not take compounding into account.

Appraisal: The monetary value of a property determined by an appraiser.

Assessment: The determined value of a property for tax purposes. A property's assessed value is multiplied by the local and state tax rates to determine the total property taxes to be paid each year.

Balloon Payment: A lump sum paid at the end of a loan's term that is significantly larger than all the payments made before it.

Base Rent: The minimum rent due each month to occupy a commercial space. The base rent does not include expenses such as property taxes, insurance, building maintenance etc.

Basis points: A unit of measurement for interest rates or yields, equal to 1/100 of a percent (0.01%).

Build Out: The work that will need to be done to make the property ready for its intended use.

Breakpoint: The point where the base rent equals the percentage rent. In other words, it's the point whereby the tenant begins paying additional rent on anything above that amount. This metric is calculated by taking the base monthly rent and dividing it by the percentage rate. For example, if a tenant signs a percentage lease with a base rent of $5,000 and a percentage rent of 7%, the sales volume breakpoint would be $71,428 per month ($5000/0.07).

Common Area Maintenance (C.A.M): The net charges billed to tenants in a commercial triple-net (NNN) lease to maintain the common areas of a commercial property. These areas may include shared hallways, bathrooms, parking lots, elevators etc.

Common Area Maintenance Cap (C.A.M Cap): The maximum amount of C.A.M. expenses a tenant is responsible for paying in a given timeframe.

Closing costs: The costs incurred by sellers and buyers in the transfer of real estate ownership.

Capital Gain: The profit that results from the sale of an asset. In commercial real estate, it's the difference between the amount you paid for the property and the price you eventually sell it for.

Capitalization Rate (Cap Rate): A real estate valuation measure used to compare different real estate investments. It's calculated by taking the net operating income (N.O.I) of a property and dividing by the property value. For example, if a property produces $75,000 in N.O.I and it's listed for sale at $1,000,000, the cap rate of the property is 7.5%.

Cash Flow: The amount of cash and cash equivalents (i.e. commercial paper, treasury bills, short term government bonds, marketable securities, money market holdings etc.) being transferred into and out of a business.

Cash-on-Cash Return: A rate of return often used in real estate transactions that calculates the cash income earned on the cash invested in the property. For example, if a property produced $12,000 per year after covering operating expenses and the mortgage and your initial investment in the deal was $120,000, your cash-on-cash return would be 10% ($12,000/$120,000).

Commercial Real Estate: Buildings or land intended to generate a profit, either from business use, capital gain or rental income. Examples of commercial real estate include multifamily, office, hospitality, industrial, raw land and retail.

Common Area: Those areas that are available for common use by all tenants, groups of tenants and their invitees. In other words, it defines the *"area which is available for use by more than one person"*.

Class: A term used to define the quality of a piece of real estate. Class A properties are the newest, best located and most sought-after in a particular market while Class C properties are generally older, marginally located and in need of maintenance.

Cost of Occupancy: The costs associated with occupying a space in a commercial building. These costs may include rent, real estate taxes, personal property taxes, insurance on the building etc.

Co-Tenancy: A situation whereby more than one tenant is occupying a commercial building. This is most common in multi-tenant properties such as strip-centers, office buildings, industrial complexes etc.

Deed: A written agreement that allows the title of a property, or an asset of some form, to be transferred from one person to another.

Demographics: Statistical data relating to the population and particular groups within it.

Depreciation: A reduction in the value of an asset with the passage of time, due to normal wear and tear.

Doing Business As (D.B.A): A business name used by companies that don't want to operate under their registered legal name.

Due Diligence: An in-depth investigation of property to confirm facts related to its acquisition. During the due diligence period, you should review financial documents, service contracts, conduct tenant interviews as well as a host of other materials.

Effective Rent: The remaining cash a landlord receives after paying all expenses for operating the property. For example, if a tenant leases a space for $3,000 per month and the landlord is responsible for covering operating expenses of $1,000 per month, their effective rent for the space would be $2,000 per month.

Environmental Hazards: Something that has the potential to threaten the surrounding natural environment and/or affect people's health. In commercial real estate, the most common environmental hazards include underground gas tanks, dry cleaning chemicals, toxic waste, sewage run-off etc.

Equity: The difference between your loan amount and the market value of your property.

Exclusivity: Allows a tenant to use the premises for a specific use (i.e. restaurant, men's apparel, nail salon etc.) and restricts other tenants from pursuing a similar use.

Expense Stop: A fixed amount of operating expense above which the tenant is responsible to pay. For example, if the landlord is responsible for paying all operating expenses for a space up to $500 per month, any expenses above that amount will become the responsibility of the tenant.

Feasibility Analysis: An investigation whose purpose is to determine the viability of purchasing a commercial property.

Fixed Costs: Expenses that are constant, regardless of the quantity. Examples of fixed costs include rent, real estate taxes and insurance.

Flex Space: Used to describe a combination of light industrial and office space.

Foundation: The support that a building rests on. These usually consist of slab, crawlspace, or basement foundations.

Free Rent: A period where rent payments are not collected. Generally, it's an incentive that landlords offer financially strong tenants to encourage them to sign a long-term lease in their commercial space.

Full-Service Gross (FSG) Lease: A lease whereby the tenant pays a base rent and the landlords covers all operating expenses related to the tenant's occupancy of the space such as common area maintenance, utilities, property insurance, and property taxes.

Gap Analysis: The difference between supply and demand of commercial real estate. This calculated by subtracting the tenant demand for space (measured in SF) by the amount of available SF of space in the market. A negative number signifies oversaturation while a positive number represents excess demand.

Gross Area: The total area within the walls of a building structure, including the walls themselves and *"unlivable"* space.

Gross Lease: A commercial lease where the tenant is responsible for paying a flat rental amount while the landlord is responsible for paying costs associated with property ownership including, but not limited to, taxes, utilities, water etc.

Gross Rent Multiplier (GRM): A ratio of the price of a real estate investment compared to its annual rental income before expenses. Investors use the GRM to determine the number of years it would take for a property to pay for itself based on its yearly gross rent.

Ground Lease: An agreement in which a tenant is permitted to develop a piece of property on the land they are renting.

Heating, Ventilation, and Air Conditioning (HVAC): A term used to describe the equipment used to keep buildings at a comfortable temperature.

Highest and Best Use: The optimal use for the property and/or space. For example, the highest and best use for a building in a high traffic area that has a grease trap, commercial kitchen hood and a drive thru is likely a restaurant.

Hold Over Fees – Fees charged to a tenant if they remain on site after their lease expiration date. Generally, these fees are added on to your base rent and range anywhere between 25-100% of your monthly rent.

Hold Over Tenant: A tenant who remains on the premises after the expiration date of the lease. If this occurs, hold-over fees are generally assessed on top of their base rent payments.

Interest rate: The amount paid by a borrower to a lender over a certain period of time.

Kick Out Clause: A clause that allows the tenant and/or landlord to cancel the lease after pre-determined period of time and/or if certain conditions have not been met.

Lease: A legally binding document detailing the terms of a real estate agreement.

Lease Buyout: A clause that allows the tenant or landlord to break the lease by paying a pre-determined amount. Generally, this amount is equivalent to a certain number of months in rent.

Lessee: An individual or corporation who has the right to use the space outlined in their lease agreement. Also known as the *"tenant"*.

Lessor: An individual or corporation who leases property to another. Also known as the *"landlord"*.

Letter of Intent (LOI): A document that declares a preliminary commitment of one party to do business with another based on an agreement of a particular set of terms. This is a non-binding document.

Load Factor: The percentage of space on a floor or building that is not usable. This ratio is expressed by taking the rentable area divided by usable area minus one.

Market Analysis: The activity of gathering information about conditions that affect a marketplace. Used to assess the suitability of a location for a given purpose.

Market Rates: The average asking rents for a particular property type based on other properties in the market.

Market Value: The most probable price a property can be sold for in a given market.

Maturity: The date when a note or a principal obligation becomes due and payable (its term ends).

Metropolitan Statistical Area (MSA): An area containing a substantial population nucleus, together with adjacent communities having a high degree of economic and social integration. In other words, it's the area in and around a city or town.

Moving Allowance: A pre-determined amount a landlord or owner will pay to cover a tenant's moving expenses.

Net lease: A lease in which the tenant pays all operating expenses in addition to rent (i.e. taxes insurance, maintenance.)

Net Operating Income: A calculation used to describe the profitability of an income producing real estate investment as well as its potential value. A property's NOI is calculated by taking its revenue and subtracting a market vacancy rate as well as reasonably necessary operating expenses.

Occupancy Cost: The costs associated with occupying a space. These expenses include, but are not limited to, rent, real estate taxes, personal property taxes, insurance on building contents etc.

Operating Expenses: The expenses associated with keeping a building operational. These expenses include, but are not limited to, utilities, water, cleaning, accounting, capital expenditures, repairs and maintenance etc.

Option: A clause within a lease agreement that allows a tenant to renew their lease for a set period of time under pre-determined terms.

Pass-Through Lease: A contract where specified operating expenses *"pass through"* from the landlord to the tenant. These additional expenses can include any combination of property taxes, insurance, maintenance, repairs and utilities.

Percentage Lease: A lease that requires a tenant to pay a base rent plus a percentage of monthly sales volume above a *"breakpoint"*.

Points: A loan discount used to adjust the yield on a loan. Points may adjust a loan to what market conditions demand.

Potential Rental Income: The amount of rent a property could generate if it was 100% occupied and leased at market rates.

Principal: The amount borrowed or the amount still owed on a loan, separate from the interest.

Property Type: The classification of commercial real estate based on its primary use. Commercial property types include multifamily, office, industrial, retail, hospitality and land.

Rate of Return: The net gain or loss of an investment over a specified time period. This metric is expressed as a percentage of the investment's initial cost.

Real Estate Cycles: A sequence of recurrent events reflected in demographic, economic and emotional factors that affect supply and demand for property. These cycles either have a negative or positive impact on the property markets.

Refinance: Replacing an old loan with a newer loan, generally offering better terms.

Rent Concessions: A period of free or reduced rent afforded to the tenant by the landlord.

Rent Escalators: Language included within a commercial lease agreement whereby operating expenses, base rent, and/or taxes may increase at pre-determined times. These increases are either monetary intervals (i.e. $50, $100, $150 etc.) or percentage intervals (i.e. 2%, 3%, 4% etc.)

Replacement Cost: The amount it would take to replace a property at the present time.

Second Generation Space: A property that was occupied by a previous tenant and was built out for their use.

Site Analysis: A process used to assess the feasibility of a property for a given use based on characteristics including, but not limited to, zoning, traffic counts, demographics, nearby suppliers etc.

Site Selection: A process used to identify the best site given a desired use.

Square Feet: A unit of measurement used in commercial real estate to describe the floor area of a space. For example, if a space were 50 feet wide and 50 ft deep, the square footage of the space would equal 2,500 SF (50 ft x 50 ft).

Sublease: The leasing of a property to a subtenant by the existing tenant. This event occurs when a tenant would like to get out of their existing lease but is unable to break the lease outright. If a *"sublease"* clause is included in the lease agreement, the tenant has the right to lease the space to another tenant barring the landlord's approval.

Tenant: An individual or business that occupies land or property owned by a landlord.

Tenant Improvement Allowance (T.I.A): The amount a landlord is willing to spend on renovating a space to fit the use of a new tenant. This metric is usually expressed on a per square foot basis.

Triple-net lease: A lease agreement whereby the tenant is responsible for paying all the expenses of the property including real estate taxes, building insurance, and maintenance.

Turnkey: A fully renovated property that a tenant can move into without any modifications.

Useable Square Feet: The total square feet of an area that is unique to the tenant and is not accessible to other tenants on the premises.

Variable Expenses: Costs that change over time. In a commercial real estate setting, these expenses may include utilities, water, trash removal, cleaning, repairs, and maintenance etc.

Zoning: Municipal or local laws or regulations that dictate how a piece of real estate can and cannot be used in certain geographic areas. This designation will determine if a property is considered commercial, residential etc.

Made in the USA
Monee, IL
28 December 2022

23968495R00085